CHARLES DICKENS
AT HOME

Hilary Macaskill

Special photography by Graham Salter

CHARLES DICKENS
AT HOME

F

FRANCES LINCOLN LIMITED
PUBLISHERS

Frances Lincoln Limited
4 Torriano Mews
Torriano Avenue
London NW5 2RZ
www.franceslincoln.com

Charles Dickens At Home
Copyright © Frances Lincoln Limited 2011
Text copyright © Hilary Macaskill 2011
Illustrations copyright as listed on page 144
First Frances Lincoln edition 2011

A catalogue record for this book is available
from the British Library.

978-0-7112-3227-3

Printed and bound in China

9 8 7 6 5 4 3 2 1

ENDPAPERS:
FRONT: The churchyard in Bowes,
setting for Dotheboys Hall in Nicholas
Nickleby, where the gravestones inspired
Dickens.
BACK: The river Thames at Wapping.

PAGE 1 The docks at Limehouse.

PAGE 2 Charles Dickens at home.

RIGHT David Copperfield of Dickens's
eponymous novel boarding the Royal
Mail coach on his way to school, in an
illustration by J. Maitand.

CONTENTS

Foreword **6**
Timeline **7**

CHILDHOOD
Portsmouth, Blundeston and Chatham 1812–22 ..... **8**

GROWING UP
London 1822–36 ..... **26**

MARRIAGE AND DOMESTICITY
1836–51 ..... **38**

DICKENS AWAY
In Britain **64**

A MAN OF MEANS
1851–60 ..... **74**

DICKENS AWAY
Abroad **90**

HOUSEHOLDS AND SERVANTS **102**

HOME AGAIN TO KENT
1860–70 ..... **114**

THE LEGACY **130**

Select Bibliography **140**
Further Information **140**
Index **141**
Acknowledgments **144**

FOREWORD

BY DR FLORIAN SCHWEIZER
DIRECTOR OF THE CHARLES DICKENS MUSEUM, LONDON

Among Charles Dickens's many skills, his ability to re-invent his own public image for almost every decade of his life is one very pertinent to this book: from the disillusioned youth of the 1820s to the radical author of the 1830s, from the international celebrity in the 1840s to the respectable gentleman and august citizen of the 1850s and 1860s, the Victorian author was able to engage his audiences throughout his career. The special bond with his readers is at the heart of his continuing appeal as a writer and cultural figure even today, and in many ways the idea of 'home' plays an important role in his relationship with the public.

As a novelist Dickens invented homes for a living. His novels are filled with domestic settings that are recognized by readers around the world, ranging from the genteel urban environment of Mr Brownlow's home in Pentonville, London, in *Oliver Twist* to Miss Havisham's gothic rural pile Satis House in *Great Expectations*. As Hilary Macaskill points out in the opening chapter to this book, 'fiction and reality merge' in Dickens's works, and many homes described in the novels are based on buildings the author had seen, visited or even lived in. Like no other writer, Dickens turns buildings, real or imagined, into homes by filling them with the characters and stories of his imagination.

But Dickens also created homes around his own life story. As a boy he was filled with a vision that a house in Kent, called Gad's Hill Place, might be his home one day if he would only work hard enough; this vision remained with him until, in 1856, he purchased the house and lived in it until his death in 1870. When his father's debts required Dickens's family to live in a debtors' prison in 1824 he felt so ashamed of his dysfunctional family home that he invented a fake one when a friend insisted on accompanying him home after work. Later in life, now a major philanthropist and social campaigner, he set up a 'Home for Homeless Women' and started up a new type of retirement homes for distinguished but impoverished artists and writers who were members of his Guild of Literature and Arts project. Despite, or perhaps because of, the constant moving from one place to another, the concept of home was an extremely important one to Dickens.

As an author whose personal experience of family home ranged from the debtors' prison to the dream country mansion, Dickens instilled into all his fiction ideals of exemplary domesticity as well as a genuine connectedness to a wide spectrum of life experiences. And whilst Dickens re-invented his own public image through the decades, these qualities sustained and strengthened his bond with the public, securing him a unique place in the hearts, minds and – through his books – by the firesides of his readers – a place, for the writer Charles Dickens, like no other: a place he could call home.

TIMELINE

	1812	7 February: Charles Dickens is born in Portsmouth.
	1815	The Dickens family moves to London.
	1817	They move to Chatham in Kent.
	1822	They move to London.
	1824	John Dickens is arrested for debt and sent to Marshalsea Prison. Charles is sent to work at Warren's blacking factory.
	1825–7	Charles attends Wellington House Academy.
	1827	Starts his first job as a lawyer's clerk.
	1831	Becomes a reporter.
	1833	Begins to write sketches and stories.
	1834	Moves into Furnival's Inn.
Sketches by Boz; The Pickwick Papers	**1836**	Marries Catherine Hogarth in Chelsea.
Oliver Twist	**1837**	Becomes editor of *Bentley's Miscellany* (until 1839). First son, Charles (Charley) Culliford, born. Moves to 48 Doughty Street. Mary Hogarth dies.
Nicholas Nickleby	**1838**	First daughter, Mary (Mamie), born.
	1839	Second daughter, Catherine (Katie) Macready, born. Moves to 1 Devonshire Terrace.
The Old Curiosity Shop	**1840**	Starts a weekly periodical, *Master Humphrey's Clock* (ceases in 1841).
Barnaby Rudge	**1841**	Tours Scotland. Son Walter Savage Landor born. Georgina Hogarth moves in.
American Notes; Martin Chuzzlewit	**1842**	Visits America with Catherine for six months.
A Christmas Carol	**1843**	
The Chimes	**1844**	Son Francis Jeffrey born. In July moves his family to Genoa for a year.
	1845	Forms amateur dramatics company. Son Alfred D'Orsay Tennyson born.
Pictures from Italy; Dombey and Son	**1846**	Becomes editor of *Daily News* for eighteen days. The family moves to Lausanne, and then winters in Paris.
	1847	Urania Cottage, 'a Home for Fallen Women', financed by Angela Burdett Coutts, opens. Son Sydney Smith Haldimand born.
David Copperfield	**1849**	Son Henry Fielding born.
	1850	Launches the weekly journal *Household Words*. Third daughter, Dora Annie, born.
	1851	Dora dies. Moves to Tavistock House.
Bleak House	**1852**	Last son, Edward Bulwer Lytton (Plorn), born.
	1853	Gives first public reading, for the Birmingham Industrial and Literary Institute.
Hard Times	**1854**	
Little Dorrit	**1855**	
	1856	Buys Gad's Hill Place in Kent.
	1857	Stages and then performs in *The Frozen Deep*, at Tavistock House and later in Manchester, where he meets actress Ellen Ternan.
	1858	Embarks on the first of his public reading tours. Separates from Catherine.
A Tale of Two Cities	**1859**	Closes *Household Words* and launches *All the Year Round*.
Great Expectations	**1860**	Sells Tavistock House and moves to Gad's Hill Place.
The Uncommercial Traveller	**1861**	
Our Mutual Friend	**1864**	
	1867–8	Visits America for reading tour.
	1868–9	Makes farewell reading tour in Britain. 22 April: collapses at Preston and cancels rest of tour.
The Mystery of Edwin Drood (unfinished)	**1870**	Gives farewell readings in London. 8 June: suffers stroke at Gad's Hill Place. 9 June: dies.

CHILDHOOD:
PORTSMOUTH, BLUNDESTON AND CHATHAM
1812–22

I was born at Portsmouth, an English seaport town, principally remarkable for mud, Jews, and Sailors, on the 7th of February 1812. My father holding in those days a situation under Government in the Navy Pay Office, which called him in the discharge of his duties to different places, I came to London, a child of two years old, left it again at six for another Sea Port town – Chatham, in the county of Kent – where I remained some six or seven years.

Thus Charles Dickens succinctly described his childhood in a letter written in 1838 to one Herr Kuenzel, who had asked him for particulars about himself for the German publication *Konversationslexikon*. His description is not entirely accurate, as he was only ten when he left Chatham, but his response emphasizes the seaside connection of his early homes and also summarizes the peripatetic nature of his childhood, a pattern

Rochester Castle, seen from the precincts of Rochester Cathedral.

that he was to repeat for the rest of his life.

To anyone who has read *David Copperfield* this synopsis may come as a shock. In this novel, recognized to be the most autobiographical, the young David Copperfield had been born in 'Blunderstone', a village between Lowestoft in Suffolk and Great Yarmouth in Norfolk. Charles Dickens describes in evocative detail the house where David lived, the Rookery:

I see the outside of our house, with the latticed bedroom-windows standing open to let in the sweet-smelling air, and the ragged old rooks'-nests still dangling in the elm-trees at the bottom of the front garden. Now I am in the garden at the back, beyond the yard where the empty pigeon-house and dog-kennel are – a very preserve of butterflies, as I remember it, with a high fence, and a gate and padlock; where the fruit clusters on the trees, riper and richer than fruit has ever been since, in any other garden, and where my mother gathers some in a basket, while I stand by, bolting furtive gooseberries, and trying to look unmoved.

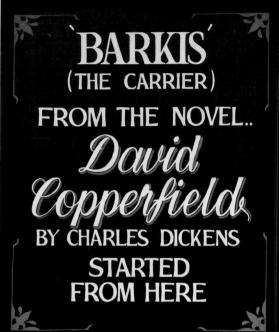

From the Rookery, there is a clear view to the round-towered church with the family pew, as David remembers: 'Here is our high-backed pew! With a window near it, out of which our house can be seen.' So vivid and precise are these descriptions, filtered through the perception of a young child, that it seems impossible that Dickens was not recollecting his own childhood home. Yet he never actually visited Blundeston at all – something that visitors (and some residents) may not appreciate.

The nearest he apparently came to the village was a signpost to it. In January 1849, just after New Year, on one of his frequent forays from the capital he had made a brief expedition with friends, John Leech and Mark Lemon, to Norfolk. Their initial goal had been Stanfield Hall, near Wymondham – which was in the news because the owner had been murdered there a few weeks previously – followed by Norwich, which they had found rather dull. So they had moved on to stay in the Royal Hotel, Great Yarmouth, which had been much more to Dickens's liking. The

next day, he had walked with Leech and Lemon to Lowestoft, 'a fine place', and back again. As he wrote subsequently to a friend, Lavinia Watson, he saw the name Blundeston on a signpost between Lowestoft and Yarmouth. To another friend, William de Cerjat, he said he had chosen it 'for the sound of its name'. There is no evidence at all that he actually visited the village, yet from this casual contact came, later that year, the seemingly authentic description of the birthplace of David Copperfield.

So steeped is Blundeston in *David Copperfield* associations that it seems inconceivable that Dickens did not know it. Streets and houses are named after his characters; the house so clearly the model for the Rookery, visible from the church, just as David says; the Plough Inn with its Dickens memorabilia and sign over the door, '"Barkis" the carrier, from the novel *David Copperfield* by Charles Dickens, started from here'. (For a period in the 1980s there was, paradoxically, an additional sign, 'No Coaches'.) On the village sign, the young David is pictured

The Dickensian Village of **BLUNDESTON** Near Lowestoft

C.W. Walker 1928

The Church (with 10th Century round tower) so freely mentioned in "David Copperfield," & famous sundial above West Door

"The Plough Inn," from here Mr. Barkis, the old carrier, started on his journeys

"The Rookery" Mrs. Copperfield's Bedroom on extreme left

Charles Dickens 1812–1870

OPPOSITE LEFT The round-towered church at Blundeston, the village where David Copperfield was born.

OPPOSITE RIGHT The sign above the door of the Plough Inn in Blundeston.

LEFT A tea towel depicting the *David Copperfield* associations.

looking towards the church. As if one needed any more proof, there are tea towels and pictures of the village mapping out the David Copperfield landmarks.

But of course the intimate portrayal from a child's viewpoint of a traditional English village, which seems utterly factual and historical wonderfully exemplifies Dickens's skill; and it demonstrates too the way a place then associated with that fictional viewpoint refashions itself in that image. Fiction and reality merge, and the end result is a village that seems to project the image created by Dickens himself.

Over the years since, a number of local guide books and articles by local historians have recorded Dickens's stay in East Anglia in detail, with anecdotes about events that could not possibly have happened in his very brief visit to the area. In the 1960s Philip Collins, an eminent Dickens scholar, wrote to the *Lowestoft Journal* in a spirit of scepticism about some of the claims surrounding Dickens's visit, and recounted that subsequently 'its editor and I received letters from various old inhabitants whose grandfathers or great-aunts recalled seeing him at the local flower show or in the

RIGHT The house at Mile End Terrace in Portsmouth where John and Elizabeth Dickens first set up home.

BELOW The bedroom where Charles Dickens was born on 7 February 1812.

OPPOSITE The parlour at the Charles Dickens' Birthplace Museum in Portsmouth, restored to the way it might have looked when the Dickens family lived there.

local pub'. He added, philosophically, that 'it is as impossible to absolutely disprove as to account for all those stories, but they are highly improbable'.

The village website doggedly adheres to the local belief: 'All we can say is that being so close in Yarmouth, it is unlikely that Dickens would have avoided the opportunity to visit. It is also apparent from the novel that he was familiar with some local landmarks such as the view of the church and the yew trees from the Rookery and the Plough Inn.'

A different aspect of this fusing of reality and fiction can be seen in the house where Dickens was actually born on 7 February 1812. This was in Landport, now on the edge of Portsmouth. Mile End Terrace is now a pretty, partially cobbled backwater of a street, tucked away behind the dual carriageway that has lopped off the ends of the terrace's gardens. The house was a new one, owned by neighbour William Pearce. The Charles Dickens' Birthplace Museum (in what has been renamed Old Commercial Road) gives an admirable and absorbing impression of the life his

John Dickens, father of Charles Dickens, as portrayed
in an etching by S. Hayden.

Elizabeth Dickens, mother of Charles Dickens, a portrait by John W. Gilbert.

family might have experienced there, and of its contents, from the cot in the corner of what was his parents' bedroom to the stove in the kitchen. His father, John Dickens, was a clerk at the Navy Pay Office, earning a salary of £111 a year; the rent for the house was £8 10s. a quarter.

John Dickens had probably gained his post through the connections of his parents: his father had been the butler at Crewe Hall in Cheshire (he died before Charles was born) and his mother the housekeeper there. It is likely that the patronage of John Crewe led to John Dickens's first post at Somerset House

in London, where he met Thomas Barrow and, through him, his sister Elizabeth. John and Elizabeth married in 1809 at the church of St Mary-le-Strand, opposite Somerset House, and their daughter Frances, known as Fanny, was born in 1810 – the same year that Elizabeth's father, Charles Barrow, who also worked at the Navy Pay Office, though in a much superior position, was found guilty of embezzlement and absconded to the Isle of Man. Despite the scandalous associations, the first son born to John and Elizabeth – in 1812, at John's new posting in Portsmouth – was named after his grandfather.

In fact, the baby Charles, along with his parents and elder sister, Fanny, lived in Mile End Terrace for only five months before moving to another house, now demolished, in Portsmouth. The only items in the Birthplace Museum that date from the period of their residence there are in the basement kitchen – the stove, and the plain painted wood dresser which forms part of the supporting wall between the kitchen and its neighbour in the terrace. But the spirit of the house has been scrupulously recreated, with the wallpaper in parlour and dining room copied from original wallpaper found during refurbishment; blue-and-white cups and plates of the sort the young couple Elizabeth and John might have used; a four-poster bed of the style that was common at that time; and pictures that they might have chosen to hang on the walls.

In June that year, the family was uprooted, moving to another, cheaper, lodging in Hawk Street, closer to the dockyard. A few months after that, their home was 39 Wish Street (now King's Road) in Southsea, which was then a new suburb – the first houses, for skilled workers, were built in 1809 – and considered to be rather superior, and with a higher rent. The fluctuations of fortune that would attend the Dickens family were already in evidence. Dickens, as he related to his friend and first biographer John Forster, could clearly remember the small front garden at Wish Street, with its gravelled path – though he was then barely two years old. He told Forster how 'he trotted about with something to eat, and his little elder sister with him'.

In January 1815, the family was on the move again, when John Dickens was recalled to London. This first period of Charles's residence in London is cloudy and undocumented. If he had particular memories of the dwelling there – near Fitzroy Square, above a greengrocer's shop in Norfolk Street (now Cleveland Street) – he did not record them. What had a far stronger impact on his childhood – and stayed with him all his life – was his father's next posting to the Royal Naval Dockyard at Chatham, at the mouth of the River Medway and close to Rochester. This area provided the settings for his first novel and for his last.

The boyhood home of Dickens in Chatham at 2 Ordnance Terrace (now renumbered as 11), on the slopes of Fort Pitt Hill.

The Dickens family's initial lodging is said to have been in Sheerness, next to a theatre, but the family's first known home in Chatham was at 2 Ordnance Terrace – now in the mysterious ways of street locations renumbered as 11. It was one of a row of new dwellings on the lower slopes of Fort Pitt Hill in what Dickens later described as 'an airy and pleasant part of the parish'. An advertisement for the house discovered by a contributor to the journal *The Dickensian* described it as a 'valuable brick built DWELLING HOUSE with yard and garden, beautifully situated, commanding beautiful views of the surrounding country, and fit for the residence of a genteel family'. The rent was £16, reduced to £15 10s. The three-storey house had a flight of steps up to the front door, a narrow hall and a collection of six rooms, which would have contained a household, by then, of eight: mother and father, mother's widowed sister (Mary Allen), three children and two servants.

But the location was good and the view from the windows would have been across fields to the River Medway and the masts of sailing ships in the dockyard. In front of the house there was a hayfield, a place for picnics and games.

Now the view is across trees bordering the railway line that replaced the field. But one can still appreciate the wonderful openness of the surroundings. Up the road, and somewhere that must have been very familiar to Charles and his sister, is the smooth sward of Fort Pitt Hill with its views across many settings that occur in Dickens's books. From here, the site for the planned duel in *The Pickwick Papers*, one can see where the prison hulks from *Great Expectations* would have skulked in the Medway; and David Copperfield walked through this scene on his way to find his aunt in Dover. The river would have etched itself on Dickens's memory – indeed the river theme recurs in his novels, though it is the River Thames that takes centre stage.

LEFT Marshes near Lower Halstow on the banks of the River Medway, evoking the setting Dickens described in *Great Expectations*.

OPPOSITE LEFT The Admiral's Building and Clock Tower at Chatham Dockyard, where John Dickens worked as a clerk in the Navy Pay Office.

OPPOSITE RIGHT The door of the Navy Pay Office, with plaques placed by descendants of Dickens.

One other significant influence of this period is recounted by Forster in his *Life of Charles Dickens* and also referred to in *David Copperfield*: that of literature. 'My father had left a small collection of books in a little room upstairs to which I had access (for it adjoined my own), and which nobody else in our house ever troubled. From that blessed little room, *Roderick Random, Peregrine Pickle, Humphrey Clinker, Tom Jones, The Vicar of Wakefield, Don Quixote, Gil Blas* and *Robinson Crusoe* came out, a glorious host, to keep me company.'

Forster says this is 'literally true', and, if so, it surely must have been at Ordnance Terrace, since their next move was to a smaller

house and it is unlikely that there would have been a room to spare there. The house at 18 St Mary's Place, where they moved in 1821, was less genteel – it had only two storeys and no flight of steps – in an area called the Brook, now demolished. But it was much closer to the dockyard where John Dickens worked. Sometimes the young Charles would walk with his father to his office in what was a delightful and much grander setting, the Georgian building of the Navy Pay Office. Two plaques, one above the other, describe the connections. The first says: 'John Dickens father of Charles Dickens worked here as a Pay Clerk 1817–1822.' The lower one, rather more verbosely and informatively, says:

John Dickens, father of Charles the author, transferred from Portsmouth to Chatham in 1817. Here, as a clerk on the staff of the Navy Pay Office, he worked on the ground floor of this building until 1822.

Charles Dickens, who was born at Portsmouth on 7th February 1812, used to frequent these premises between the ages of five and eleven. Sometimes his father used to take him to Sheerness in the Pay Office yacht when going there to make payment.

The final paragraph is equally interesting: 'The adjacent plaque was put up in October 1963 during the time that Captain P.G.C. Dickens, Royal Navy, a great-grandson of the author, was Captain of the Dockyard.' It is a pleasing codicil to the Dickens connection: at least four descendants of Charles Dickens joined the Navy and served with distinction.

Now the building of what was the Navy Pay Office houses a number of offices of small companies and organizations, such as

BELOW Marshes at Cooling, the setting for Pip's meeting with the convict Magwitch in *Great Expectations*.

OPPOSITE A magic lantern show, a favourite childhood pastime of Dickens.

Age Concern; and the dockyard, which until the 1980s throbbed with activity and 10,000 personnel, has become a tourist attraction, the Historic Dockyard Chatham. Captain Peter Dickens, while he was Captain of the Dockyard, would have lived in the imposing residence opposite, erected in 1895. The fine terrace of houses, built in 1722–3, round the corner from the Pay Office, and on a bank overlooking the dockyard and the water, provided the very grand tied cottages of the most privileged workers – the Master Shipwright, Clerk of the Cheque, Storekeeper, Master Caulker and Surgeon.

Charles Dickens would have been familiar with all this, and later wrote about the dockyard in *The Uncommercial Traveller*. On boat journeys with his father to Sheerness to pay the sailors, he would have seen, perhaps at close quarters, the convicts on prison ships, as well as the marshes at Cooling from which – many decades later – arose the story of Pip in another semi-autobiographical novel, *Great Expectations*, though of a more chastened self. As Dickens wrote: 'We received our earliest and most enduring impressions among barracks and soldiers, and ships and sailors.'

The time Charles spent in this town was a happy period, which set the foundation for his life. It is in Chatham that his real childhood memories begin, and these created the basis of his strong sense of home and family that infused his fiction and became so closely associated with Charles Dickens the author. This was, for him, his home town.

Mary Weller, who was a servant in the Dickens household in Chatham, recalled a happy and lively household. Born in 1804 – and therefore only eight years older than Charles – she was as much a companion in his endeavours as a servant. 'Sometimes Charles would come downstairs and say to me, "Now Mary, clear the kitchen, we are going to have such a game."' As she recollected, on some such occasions, their neighbour George Stroughill would come in with his magic lantern 'and they would sing, recite, and perform parts of plays. Fanny and Charles often sang together

at this time, Fanny accompanying on the pianoforte.' Mary also recollected that Charles was taught to read by his aunt and mother, 'a dear good mother, and a fine woman'.

The young Charles learned to declaim here. His favourite piece for recitation was 'The Voice of the Sluggard' by Dr Isaac Watts, 'and the little boy used to give it with great effect, and with such action and such attitudes'. It's a fitting text, as the chief characteristic of Charles Dickens throughout his life was as far removed from idleness as it is possible to imagine. The first and last verses of this are as follows:

> 'Tis the voice of the sluggard; I heard him complain,
> You have waked me too soon, I must slumber again;
> As the door on its hinges, so he on his bed
> Turns his sides and his shoulders and his heavy head. . . .
>
> Said I then to my heart, 'Here's a lesson for me,'
> This man's but a picture of what I might be:
> But thanks to my friends for their care in my breeding,
> Who taught me betimes to love working and reading.

Sometimes he would go with his father into Rochester: his father was friendly with the landlord of the Mitre Tavern, which is where he got his first taste of performing in public – a crucially important part of his later life – when he was put on the table to sing duets with his sister to acclaim. It was a precursor of his exuberant enjoyment of the theatricals he staged in later life.

His lifelong interest in the theatre was stimulated by the family's new lodger, James Lamert, the stepson of Mrs Dickens's sister, who had married again: he took a kindly interest in the young Charles, and often took him to the Theatre Royal in Rochester. Lamert was later to play a much more negative, though key, role in the development of Charles Dickens the author, but these excursions provided the boy with a bedrock of enthusiasm: there was not only

OPPOSITE The 'queer old clock' in Rochester High Street, as Dickens described it in the story 'The Seven Poor Travellers'.

LEFT The magnificent Guildhall Chamber in Rochester, model for the town hall where Pip in *Great Expectations* became an apprentice to Joe Gargery.

BELOW The dark-panelled upper room of Eastgate House, Rochester, which features as the Nuns' House in *The Mystery of Edwin Drood*.

the delight of watching the play but also, no doubt, a growing awareness of the shortcomings of productions and the inadequacy of some aspirant actors (later recalled in the parish clerk Wopsle's doomed attempts to play Hamlet, in *Great Expectations*) as well as the melodrama on which he often relied in his fiction. Theatre would provide a much-needed escape from real life and became a focus of much of his activity in his later life.

The landmarks of Rochester became part of Dickens's imagination: the Bull coaching inn that, with its accolade 'good house – nice beds', provided the first overnight stop for Pickwickians in *The Pickwick Papers* and was the Blue Boar in *Great Expectations*; Eastgate House, a magnificent Elizabethan house which featured in his first novel, as Westgate House, and his last, as the Nuns' House, a school for young ladies; as well as, of course, the cathedral and the castle, which last held a particular place in his affections. One memorable visit to Rochester, much later in life, was to the castle, with his American publisher James Fields, who recalled: 'We climbed up the time-worn walls and leaned out of the ivied windows ... That day he seemed to revel in the past. We lived over again with him many a chapter in the history of Rochester.'

Rochester today strongly resembles the town of Dickens's time. The castle and cathedral are recognizable from the description given by 'the stranger' (Jingle) in the Pickwickians' coach: 'glorious pile – frowning walls – tottering arches – dark nooks – crumbling staircases – old cathedral too – earthy smell – pilgrims' feet wore away the old steps – little Saxon doors – confessionals like money-takers' boxes at theatres'. One very evident change, however, is the prevalence of Dickensian names that have been bestowed on establishments: Peggoty's Parlour tea rooms, Copperfield's antique dealers, Nickleby's card shop, Pips of Rochester greengrocer, Little Dorrit Revival ethnic clothing.

Throughout his adult life, Dickens returned here often, sometimes on excursions with friends (in 1847 he stayed at

OPPOSITE The nave of Rochester Cathedral.

BELOW Rochester Castle behind Minor Canon Row, a row of eighteenth-century houses built for the clergy of the cathedral.

Illustration for Dickens's story 'The Seven Poor Travellers'.

the Bull – by then the Royal Victoria and Bull Hotel, after an overnight stay by the Princess Victoria in 1836), and always finding material for his novels and for his journalism, such as an article on Chatham in his magazine *Household Words* in 1853, 'When We Stopped Growing', and the short story 'The Seven Poor Travellers' in the 1854 Christmas number, based on the Six Poor Travellers almshouse set up by a charity of the sixteenth-century MP Sir Richard Watts – and still functioning.

The young Dickens's home of Chatham became Mudfog in *The Uncommercial Traveller,* and in *David Copperfield* it appeared under its real name: 'Chatham, – which, in that night's aspect, is a mere dream of chalk, and drawbridges, and mastless ships in a muddy river, roofed like Noah's arks.' Rochester became Dullborough in *The Uncommercial Traveller* and is Cloisterham in his last, unfinished novel, *The Mystery of Edwin Drood.*

The surrounding countryside provided inspiration, as well as precious memories, such as the energetic and companionable walks with his father. It was on one of these walks through Higham that he first noted the red-brick mansion with bell-tower at Gad's Hill Place. 'And ever since I can recollect,' he wrote in *The Uncommercial Traveller,* 'my father, seeing me so fond of it, has often said to me, "If you were to be very persevering and were to work hard, you might some day come to live in it . . . "' As indeed he did.

The walks through the countryside of Kent remained with Dickens as an ideal of good English life, and he often returned in adult life for similar excursions, before he came back to live in the neighbourhood. He recalled, much later, his sister's potent memories, shortly before she died, of the smell of the fallen leaves in the woods where they had walked as children.

He attended a school in Chatham newly set up by William Giles, the son of the local Baptist minister, who had not long left Oxford. In 1822, when John Dickens was recalled to work at Somerset House, Charles stayed behind, lodging with the schoolmaster for some weeks. On the day before he left Chatham behind for good,

Giles gave him as a keepsake a copy of Oliver Goldsmith's *The Bee*, the periodical first published in 1759 – a portent for the future and Dickens's setting up of his own periodicals.

On a rainy day late in 1822 he boarded the coach for the Cross Keys Inn, Wood Street, Cheapside, as he later recounted in his essay on Rochester revisited ('Dullborough Town'). Chatham was his childhood. With his move to London, adulthood would soon be thrust upon him.

Gad's Hill Place, 'a dream of my childhood', which Dickens saw on his walks with his father, illustrated by contemporary artist Frederic Kitton.

Gadshill Place

GROWING UP:
LONDON
1822–36

Pip in *Great Expectations* made the same journey to London as the young Charles Dickens. Pip alighted from the coach at the Cross Keys Inn (long gone):

The journey from our town to the metropolis, was a journey of about five hours. It was a little past mid-day when the four-horse stage-coach, by which I was a passenger, got into the ravel of traffic frayed out about the Cross Keys, Wood-street, Cheapside, London.

Dickens's arrival in London was not his first, the family having lived here for nearly two years before John Dickens's job took him to Chatham, but he was an infant then, and in later life divulged

The London to Brighton Coach at Cheapside, painted by William Turner in 1831, shows the sort of scenes Dickens (and Pip) would have encountered when he arrived in London.

no memories of this time. His return in 1822 was the beginning of an intense relationship with the capital, then a city much smaller than our conception of it, or, indeed, the Victorian metropolis we associate with Dickens. London was the background for many of his books, and seemed to play a part as big as any of his characters; it was 'the real hero of Dickens's novels . . . his closest friend and dearest enemy', as the critic Peter Quennell described it.

Dickens came to know London very well in his years of living there and on his long walks around all districts, and he was for years passionately committed to the city. When, decades later, he was living in Lausanne, he longed for an urban environment, to walk along streets, to be in London. 'A day in London sets me up and starts me,' he wrote to John Forster. But foreign residence changed his attitude to London: in February 1851, he wrote: 'I have never taken kindly to it, since I lived abroad. Whenever I come back from the country, now, and see that great heavy canopy lowering over the house tops, I wonder what on earth I do there except on obligation.' Nevertheless, London remained

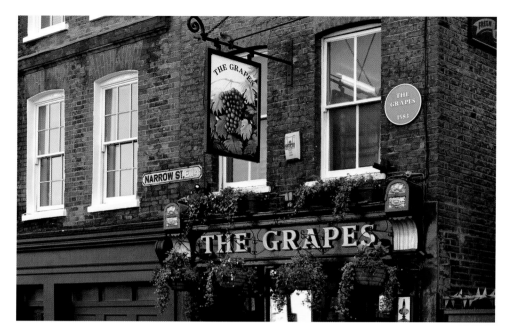

16 Bayham Street, Dickens's first home in London.

The Grapes in Limehouse, which appears as Six Jolly Fellowship Porters in *Our Mutual Friend*.

fundamental to his art: the 'great heavy canopy' hung over the first pages of *Bleak House*, which was published the following year, and its setting of London was as important as the characters.

Despite his bitter renunciation of London – in 1856 he wrote to his wife, Catherine: 'the streets are hideous to behold, and the ugliness of London is quite astonishing' – the city retained its hold, its fascination, though the London that was so much a part of Dickens's books was not Victorian London but stemmed from the early wanderings of a pre-Victorian era. In much later years, he was able to admire wholeheartedly the new developments. In a letter to William de Cerjat, a friend he had made in Lausanne, in 1865 he approvingly described the great embankment rising 'high and dry out of the Thames on the Middlesex shore, from Westminster Bridge to Blackfriars', adding 'moreover, a great system of drainage'. Four years later, in an update, he called it 'the finest public work yet done'.

The first place he lived was not considered to be actually in London: Bayham Street is now a wide one-way route parallel to Camden High Street and inextricably part of the big city, but then Camden Town was separated from the town by fields. Forster in his *Life* describes the new family home, number 16 (demolished in 1910), as 'a mean small tenement with a wretched little back-garden abutting on a squalid court'. (Houses in this area are now considered to be quite desirable.) This no doubt derives from Charles Dickens's recollections, coloured by the start of a harsh period of his life, but other contemporary views of the mixed community of traders, professionals and artisans are less damning. The house was new – only ten years old – and being on the edge of the country, hard though that is to imagine, it had the advantages that accompanied that.

The young boy's impressions were not confined to Camden Town. There were visits to Limehouse to visit his godfather,

Christopher Huffam, a sail-maker for the Royal Navy who lived in a substantial way, and who keenly appreciated, along with his friends, the comic performing talents of the boy. It is likely that Dickens became familiar then with the Grapes, which in *Our Mutual Friend* became the Six Jolly Fellowship Porters. Even now it is just possible to imagine the pub as it might have been then, with its wooden walls, bare floorboards and steps leading to a deck over the Thames. He also visited Thomas Barrow, his mother's elder brother, who lived in Soho, in Gerrard Street, as did the lawyer Jaggers in *Great Expectations*. Happily for the young Charles, his uncle lodged over a bookshop, a fact that the boy made the most of on his visits.

In an essay for *Household Words*, many years later, Dickens wrote in 'Gone Astray' a captivating description of a day when he was, he said, lost. Whether fictional or not, it seems to have been based on an early experience of seeing the 'Giants in Guildhall' (statues of Gog and Magog), Temple Bar (that 'leaden-headed old obstruction' in *Bleak House*), and the mechanical giants striking hours at St Dunstan's in Fleet Street (later mentioned in *Barnaby Rudge*). This fascination with the wonders – and the perils – of the capital city are echoed in David Copperfield's impression that London, 'an amazing place', was 'fuller of wonders and wickedness than all the cities of the earth'.

At the end of his life it was the seamy side of London that maintained its hold on his imagination. Just as he had been fascinated by the 'rookeries' of St Giles, sometimes leading visitors to see such slums (but often paying for this voyeurism by, for example on one visit, leaving two half crowns in each room), so at the end of his life he returned to Limehouse. He took his friend and publisher James Fields there, in the company of a police inspector (such was the influence of the great novelist) to see an opium den. His final novel opens with such a scene.

Many years after he had left it, Dickens returned to write about Camden Town, much changed by the arrival of the railway. In an article for *Household Words*, he remarked with irony on all the

An opium den in the East End of London, as portrayed in the opening scene of Dickens's last novel, *The Mystery of Edwin Drood*.

changes – the Railway Hotel, the Railway Bakery, the Railway Hair-cutting Saloon: 'THE RAILROAD has done it all.' He also wrote about it in *Dombey and Son*, describing how the railway went through Staggs Gardens, 'a little row of houses, with little squalid patches of ground before them, fenced off with old doors, barrel staves, scraps of tarpaulin, and dead bushes; with bottomless tin kettles and exhausted iron fenders, thrust into the gaps. Here, the Staggs's Gardeners trained scarlet beans, kept fowls and rabbits, erected rotten summer-houses (one was an old boat), dried clothes, and smoked pipes.'

Though the overall impression conveyed is critical, there is an affectionate note which tempers his unfavourable reminiscences of it; Camden Town appears in *A Christmas Carol* as the place where the Cratchits live and celebrate their Christmas feast – surely one of the most transformative and joyful of episodes – and in *David Copperfield*, as where Mr Micawber lives in 'faded gentility'. So perhaps his memories were not all negative.

The Bayham Street home, however, marked the start of a difficult time. The house was small. By 1822, there were three

ABOVE Marshalsea Prison.

RIGHT Inscription in the paving stone next to the only remaining wall of the prison.

more children – Letitia, Frederick and Alfred – so the two-storey terraced house provided accommodation for a family of seven, as well as the maid they had brought with them from the Chatham workhouse and – most portentously – the lodger, James Lamert, who unwittingly was to bring about the worst but perhaps the most critically important episode in Dickens's life.

But first there was yet another move. In an effort to help the family finances – John Dickens was in debt – Elizabeth Dickens planned to open a school, and the family moved to 4 Gower Street North (now submerged by University College Hospital). It was an enterprising but doomed scheme. A brass plate was erected, and Charles distributed leaflets, but there were no pupils. Their stay there was not long: the debts increased, and his father was arrested and removed to Marshalsea Prison. The famous catchphrase of

Mr Micawber in *David Copperfield* derived directly from what his father had said to him sorrowfully when Charles first visited him at Marshalsea. In Dickens's own words:

He told me, I remember, to take warning by the Marshalsea, and to observe that if a man had twenty pounds a year, and spent nineteen pounds nineteen shillings and sixpence, he would be happy, but that a shilling the other way would make him wretched. I see the fire we sat before now, with two bricks inside the rusted grate, one on each side, to prevent its burning too many coals.

The depleted family struggled on for a short while at Gower Street, before they went, as many families of prisoners did, to join John Dickens in Marshalsea. All, that is, except his elder daughter, Fanny, who had escaped via a scholarship to the Royal College of Music, and Charles, who had received an offer that he could not refuse – from the former lodger James Lamert, who was working as a manager in his cousin's factory, which made blacking for boots. The offer was of a job labelling bottles for six or seven shillings a week, along with a promise of a little education from Lamert in the lunch hour. So this twelve-year-old boy, deprived of his family, was left to earn his living and to lodge in Little College Street (now College Place) near St Pancras Church in Camden Town with an old lady known to the family, Mrs Roylance: she later became Mrs Pipchin in *Dombey and Son*.

Warren's blacking factory was at Hungerford Stairs, close by Charing Cross, a site now occupied by Charing Cross station. It was a tumbledown old house, abutting the river and infested with vermin. In the fragment of autobiography he gave to John Forster in 1847, Dickens wrote 'its wainscotted rooms and its rotten floors and staircase, and the old grey rats swarming down in the cellars, and the sound of their squeaking and scuffling coming up the stairs at all times, and the dirt and decay of the place, rise visibly up before me, as if I were there again'. As if his environment were not bad enough, the educational lunch hours did not last, and so his days became ones of unremitting grinding toil. He would walk from Camden Town to his workplace, and on Sundays, would call for Fanny and trudge to Borough so that he could spend the day in Marshalsea pPrison, where Mr and Mrs Dickens and the three youngest children were living, still attended by their maid, though she lived out. For the young boy it was a wretchedly solitary existence. The despondency and hopelessness of those days stayed with him for the rest of his life.

When his distress became evident to his family, a move was organized, and he lodged thereafter in a room in Lant Street in Borough. This was an altogether happier experience, as recounted in the autobiographical fragment: 'The little window had a pleasant prospect of a timber yard, and when I took possession of my new abode, I thought it was a Paradise.' Lant Street makes an appearance in *The Pickwick Papers* and the landlord, 'a fat, good-natured, kind old gentleman', and his wife and son are affectionately remembered in *The Old Curiosity Shop*.

A sketch by Charles Fowler of Hungerford Stairs, at the edge of the River Thames, where Warren's blacking factory was located.

Dickens was, at last, close to his family, and could at least breakfast with them before going to work. The work itself remained relentlessly grim, though the enforced independence of this young boy, who wandered round places nearby, such as Covent Garden and the Adelphi, down by the Thames, had its beneficial effects for Dickens the author. Many of his experiences of this period, when he was propelled into adulthood, provided useful material: some of his characters find lodgings in the area – Arthur Clennam in Covent Garden, David Copperfield at the Adelphi, Martin Chuzzlewit in the Strand.

In 1857, he revisited the site of Marshalsea to recall his memories for *Little Dorrit*, by which time very little of it remained. He wrote in the preface: 'I almost gave up every brick of the jail for lost' until he turned into Angel Court, now Angel Place, where a

ABOVE Doyce Street, named after Arthur Clennam's partner in *Little Dorrit*, close to the site of Marshalsea.

RIGHT The public garden by the old wall of Marshalsea.

wanderer 'will find his feet on the very paving-stones of the extinct Marshalsea jail'. At one side is the battered brick wall that was the outer wall of the prison, dividing off what was the courtyard of the prison from the graveyard, now a small public garden. There's nothing much else that recalls those days of Dickens's association, except for the names of the streets around, such as Doyce Street, named after Arthur Clennam's partner.

When John Dickens managed to free himself from the Marshalsea, Dickens was reunited with his family, and he moved with them back north of the river, first of all to Little College Street. But he was not released from his bondage at the factory – until one day, some months later, his father, passing by, saw him at his work in the window of the new premises to which the factory had moved and, shocked at the sight, brought him

home instantly. Charles never quite forgave his mother who, anxious not to lose income in a household that was continually on a financial knife-edge, was, as Dickens put it, 'warm for me going back'. But his father prevailed and allowed him two years' more schooling, at Wellington House Academy, situated then on Hampstead Road, opposite a dairy farm; it was later demolished for the railway. Though he was not there long, the school left its mark: it appears as Salem House in *David Copperfield,* and its headmaster William Jones as David's brutal schoolmaster, Mr Creakle.

By this time the Dickens family was living in Johnson Street, Somers Town, in a pleasant house and for once the family was relatively settled, living there for four years. John Dickens changed career, mastering shorthand and becoming a journalist. But financial trouble erupted again, and they were evicted and briefly moved to 1 The Polygon, Somers Town, a circle of houses in Clarendon Square (where Mary Wollstonecraft had lived and her daughter Mary, author of *Frankenstein*, was born). Thence, the

A portrait of the young Charles Dickens
by his friend Daniel Maclise.

LEFT Offices in Gray's Inn, where Dickens began his first job as a lawyer's clerk.

RIGHT Staple Inn, which features in *Bleak House* and *The Mystery of Edwin Drood*.

family embarked on a dizzying round of addresses which included North Road Highgate, Fitzroy Street, 10 Norfolk Street, 3 Belle Vue Hampstead, all before the end of 1831 (when John Dickens was again declared insolvent). There was continual uncertainty in their domestic life.

When Dickens left Wellington House Academy at sixteen, he became a lawyer's clerk for a number of different sets of legal chambers – at one of which he met Thomas Mitton, who became a close friend and his solicitor for a good part of his life. Then at seventeen he became a shorthand reporter in Doctors' Commons, whose three different courts, dealing with 'wills, wives and wrecks', all provided more material for his future writing.

It was while working there, in about 1830, that he met Maria Beadnell, the pretty but fickle daughter of a banker who lived in

Lombard Street. It was his first romance – he was still in his teens – but intense, and he spent three years wooing her with letters and comic poems. However, his feelings seem to have been half-heartedly reciprocated at best, and her parents were discouraging to this young man with no prospects. Soon after his twenty-first birthday he finally broke off the affair. His passionate affection for her left a residual sadness, a feeling of rejection: an effect that somehow remained with him, though perhaps based more on a fantasy than on anything more solid. It also left him with a great sense of determination.

Perhaps spurred on by the Beadnells' disparagement of him, in 1831 he had moved on to *The Mirror of Parliament*, owned by his uncle John Barrow, which reported on parliamentary debates. By this time the Dickens family had moved to Margaret Street, behind Oxford Street, and then to Bentinck Street, but Charles had made two brief forays away, to 15 Buckingham Street, where David Copperfield lodged as a young man, and later to Cecil Street.

He worked in the House of Commons transcribing everything said in the debates. Then he began to write articles and stories for magazines and newspapers, using the nickname Boz – purloined from his youngest brother, Augustus (born in 1827), who had been nicknamed Moses but pronounced it 'Boses', and which, in the way of nicknames, was shortened and adapted. His big breakthrough came when he started writing a series of pieces for the *Morning Chronicle* and then for its offshoot, the *Evening Chronicle*, edited by George Hogarth, an early fan of the young writer. These articles were eventually gathered together and published by John Macrone as *Sketches by Boz*: the Inimitable Boz, as Dickens referred to himself at intervals throughout his life.

Lincoln's Inn gardens.

At the end of 1834, he made his first independent home. When his father was again arrested for debt, he took over the reins of the family's household, put his mother and youngest siblings into cheaper lodgings, and took himself and his favourite brother, Fred, away from the family. On 16 December 1834, he moved to Furnival's Inn into a 'three pair back' – three rooms, with a cellar and store room. Furnival's Inn no longer had any legal connections, having been redeveloped as apartments in 1818, but it retained the name and, in the public mind at any rate, an association with the law until the site was redeveloped again, in 1879, as the floridly red-brick headquarters of the Prudential

Assurance Company. Before moving into Furnival's Inn, Dickens had investigated the possibility of living in chambers at New Inn, saying that he intended entering the bar as soon as circumstances enabled him to do so. He later registered as a law student at Middle Temple, cautiously keeping the possibility of a legal profession at the back of his mind for many years.

From the seventeenth century, bachelor chambers in the Inns had become desirable dwellings for the fashionable, and they crop up in several of Dickens's novels. Sir John Chester in *Barnaby Rudge* lives in Middle Temple. Tommy Traddles in *David Copperfield* has chambers in Gray's Inn. John Westlock in *Martin Chuzzlewit* lives in Furnival's Inn. Wood Hotel, behind Furnival's Inn, and Staple Inn feature in *The Mystery of Edwin Drood*: Mr Tartar's rooms, in *Edwin Drood*, are 'the neatest, cleanest and best-ordered chambers ever seen under the sun, moon and stars. No man-of-war was ever kept more spick and span from careless touch.' Mr Snagsby in *Bleak House* loves to walk in Staple Inn in summertime 'and to observe how countrified the sparrows and leaves are'. In *Martin Chuzzlewit*, John Westlock woos Ruth Pinch in the Temple's Fountain Court: 'brilliantly the Temple Fountain sparkled in the sun, and laughingly its liquid music played, and merrily the idle drops of water danced and danced, and peeping out in sport among the trees, plunged lightly down to hide themselves'. Pip in *Great Expectations* lives with Herbert Pocket in Barnard's Inn (now part of Gresham College) – perhaps recreating Dickens's own bachelor dwelling with his brother Fred. The year before he died, he brought James Fields here to point out 'Pip's room'.

It must have been a liberating time for Dickens, free as he was temporarily from the troubled domestic cares of his family. He began the tradition of hospitality with which he would be associated for the rest of his life. He wrote to Henry Austin, an architect and engineer (and later to marry his sister Letitia), suggesting that he move in, describing as enticement a nameplate in the Inn – black on white – and asserting that 'I shall be most happy to give you free use of such furniture and appurtenances as I have . . . and make any alteration in my Chambers that you may think desirable.' This invitation was not accepted. But it did not deter Dickens from inviting friends for meals, though his environment must have been sparse for the first few months. There is an account of a visitor, one N.P. Willis, calling on him there with his publisher and friend John Macrone, who remarked on 'an uncarpeted and bleak-looking room, with a deal table, two or three chairs and a few books'. Dickens had to delay one social occasion on account of having 'no *dishes*, no curtains, no french polish', though he adds as an inducement for a later date that he had some 'really extraordinary French brandy'.

Dickens enjoyed the food and conviviality of social occasions that characterized the rest of his life – and his novels. One deliciously described meal taken by John Westlock in Furnival's Inn in *Martin Chuzzlewit* was perhaps inspired by a real-life occasion in his bachelor apartment here:

Suddenly there appeared a being in a white waistcoat, carrying under his arm a napkin, and attended by another being with an oblong box upon his head from which a banquet, piping hot, was taken out and set upon the table.

Salmon, lamb, peas, innocent young potatoes, a cool salad, sliced cucumber, a tender duckling and a tart – all there . . . He was never surprised, this man; he never seemed to wonder at the extraordinary things he found in the box, but he took them out with a face expressive of a steady purpose and impenetrable character, and put them on the table . . . dinner being done, and wine and fruit arranged upon the board, he vanished, box and all, like something that had never been.

Percy Fitzgerald, a later friend and contributor to Dickens's magazines, visited Furnival's Inn for an article in *The Dickensian*, noting probably the one thing remaining that had been there during Dickens's residence, the brass-bound stair rail up the steep dark stairs to the apartment, and he described the large hotel to the rear, Wood Hotel, which provided lodging for Rosa Budd (Rosa's room was 'airy, clean, comfortable, almost gay') in *The Mystery of Edwin Drood*.

Dickens's bachelor life did not last long. When the genial George Hogarth, editor of the *Evening Chronicle*, invited him to his Chelsea home, he promptly fell in love with his daughter, nineteen-year-old Catherine, a pretty, sweet-tempered, mild girl as far removed from Maria Beadnell as was possible. He could see in her the future of a home of settled domestic harmony.

An eighteenth-century painting by Joseph Nicholls showing Middle Temple Hall from Fountain Court.

Marriage and Domesticity: 1836–51

On 2 April 1836, Charles Dickens married Catherine Hogarth, eldest daughter of George Hogarth, at St Luke's Church in Chelsea, the newly built parish church attended by the Hogarths. He had for four months the previous year lived near by so that he could see more of his betrothed, at 11 Selwood Terrace, a prime example of late Georgian speculative housing built in 1829, in a new development owned by Samuel Ware, who built Burlington Arcade in Piccadilly. (Eighty years later, another young novelist lived briefly close by, at 9 Selwood Terrace, before *his* marriage: D.H. Lawrence, who married Frieda von Richthofen at Kensington Register Office in July 1914.) From Selwood Terrace Charles could walk the short distance to the Hogarth family home in York Place, a pleasant location opposite green-hedged market gardens (now the site of Brompton Hospital). Sometimes Catherine would walk over in the mornings (chaperoned, no doubt, by one of her younger sisters) to make an early breakfast for the young reporter. Meanwhile, he kept on his bachelor apartment at Furnival's Inn

St Luke's Church in Chelsea, where Charles Dickens married Catherine Hogarth.

in Holborn, to which he would occasionally return, usually for reasons of work, from this suburb of orchards and gardens.

He had realized soon in their relationship that the Hogarth household, though warm and friendly, was also disorganized and untidy. He needed to school Catherine, he thought, and wean her away from the bohemian muddle of her home. While staying at Selwood Terrace, he wrote many letters to her, which display a mixture of affection and instruction. He was only four years older than her, but considerably more worldly wise – and with already firm views on how life as a married couple should be. The breakfast-making was, surely, not only a convenience for him and a chance to meet but also practice for her.

By this time the young Charles Dickens was very used to organizing households: he had, after all, taken on the role of manager of his own chaotic family. He also clearly enjoyed the home-making aspect associated with the households he managed – and the shopping. Early in their relationship, for example, he had written proudly to Catherine of the preparations he had made for a visit by her and her mother and sister to Furnival's Inn, describing his purchases: 'a pair of quart decanters, and a pair of

LEFT Portraits by Samuel Laurence of Charles and Catherine Dickens.

BELOW The marriage certificate.

OPPOSITE LEFT The house in Selwood Terrace, near Catherine Hogarth's home, where Dickens lived in 1835.

OPPOSITE RIGHT Title page of *Sketches by Boz*, published in 1836 and Dickens's first success.

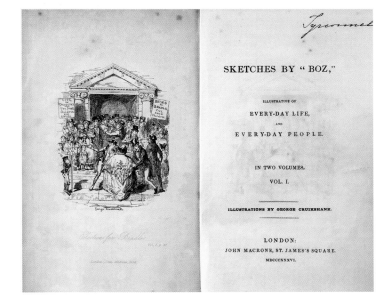

pints, a chrystal Jug and three brown dittos with plated tops, for beer and hot water, a pair of lustres [prismatic glass pendants] and two *magnificent* china Jars – all, I flatter myself, slight bargains'.

The results of his schooling must have been satisfactory, as the wedding took place sooner than they originally intended. *Sketches by Boz* was a financial success and it was clear that *The Pickwick Papers*, which he was now in the course of writing in monthly instalments, was proving popular. So, after obtaining a special marriage licence (Catherine was still a minor), they were married on a fine spring day. It was a small ceremony, attended only by

the immediate families, and three friends – John Macrone, Henry Burnett (who was later to marry Charles's older sister, Fanny) and Thomas Beard, best man, whose comment on the wedding day was that it was 'altogether a very quiet bit of business'.

Dickens's gift to his wife, suitably, was a sandalwood workbox inlaid with ivory. After the wedding breakfast at the Hogarths' house, he took his bride to the scene of his childhood contentment in Kent, to a simple whitewashed cottage in the village of Chalk. This is another of those places associated with Dickens that became muddled with the passing of time. A plaque was placed on the wall of Craddock's Cottage, stating that this was where they had spent their honeymoon, only for this to be undermined years later by research that established that he had actually stayed in another cottage, now demolished (a fate that has befallen many of the homes Dickens lived in). But whichever house it was, it was in an area for which he felt deep affection and they returned on other occasions. It is perhaps no surprise that later, in *Great Expectations,* he modelled the forge of Joe Gargery, one of the most amiable characters in his fiction, on a building in Chalk, even to the position of the connecting door between home and workplace.

CHARLES DICKENS AT HOME

After their honeymoon, they returned to London, to Furnival's Inn, where he had arranged to move from his bachelor quarters into a third-floor apartment, 'three-pair front, south, at £50 a year for three years certain' with a kitchen – and in which the landlord allowed children. This was an essential requirement, for Catherine was soon pregnant: their first son, Charles (Charley), was born on 6 January 1837.

Mary Hogarth, Catherine's younger sister and a frequent visitor, wrote to a friend about the pleasing nature of the Dickens's first home, describing it as a suite of rooms 'opening from one to another', featuring rosewood in the drawing room and mahogany in the dining room, and about Catherine's happiness as a young wife: Catherine, she said, 'makes a most capital housekeeper and is as happy as the day is long'.

Charles and, with his encouragement, Catherine enjoyed entertaining. Dickens's interest in food – his detailed and frequent references to food are one of the characteristics of his fiction – must surely have been given free rein in those early days in Furnival's Inn. They held their first big dinner party on 23 July 1836: Charles reported with animation to Catherine's grandfather, George Thomson, that Catherine had not yet quite recovered from 'the high and mighty satisfaction she derived from a supper of her own invention and arrangement' at their first party. Dinner at five o'clock, then the usual time, was followed by a reading of the libretto for a comic opera, *The Village Coquettes* – which Dickens had written for composer John Pyke Hullah – while the music was tried out on their cottage piano.

Meanwhile, he set himself a pattern of work that rarely diminished over his lifetime. After Charley's birth they went to Chalk for two months, possibly for Catherine's health, but also so that he could work without distraction, though there were occasional visits to London. As well as writing an instalment of *The Pickwick Papers* each month for Chapman and Hall, he was contributing articles to the *Morning Chronicle*. He was by now

OPPOSITE Craddock's Cottage in Chalk, with a bust of Dickens and a plaque saying that the couple honeymooned there.

ABOVE Catherine, painted in watercolour by Daniel Maclise.

editor of the literary magazine *Bentley's Miscellany* and began to read masses of manuscripts each month – sixty to eighty, he estimated – as well as editing the chosen few. And, of course, he was writing some of the articles too. The first couple he wrote were set in Mudfog, his name for Chatham; the second of these featured a young boy called Oliver Twist, born in a workhouse there: the seeds of that novel were sown. By setting the story of the runaway Oliver in the criminal underworld, Dickens could use his experience of the unsavoury streets of London. And his current home was close to the area round Saffron Hill and Field Lane, home of Fagin's nest of thieves.

Furnival's Inn appears to have been a happy home, but once a baby had arrived, the three-roomed apartment quickly proved too small. In his brief attempt at a diary in 1938, when recalling his time there, Dickens wrote: 'I shall never be so happy again as in those chambers three storeys high – never if I roll in wealth and fame. I would hire them to keep empty, if I could afford it.' He had already been keeping an eye open for a suitable house before he and Catherine were married: when visiting illustrator George Cruikshank at the end of November 1835, he had strolled about Pentonville, looking at houses in the new streets, but he had found them expensive for their size: the cheapest he could find then was £55 a year.

By February 1937 he was house-hunting again – at least once with his sister-in-law, Mary. He sometimes went shopping with her too, as he recalled the following year: on the day of Charley's birth they had, he said, wandered round Holborn and the streets about for hours, looking for a little table for Catherine's bedroom. They found one eventually; they had seen it at the start of their search, but he hadn't liked to ask the price – an odd display of reticence for Dickens. He could exhibit considerable patience and determination in acquiring items: later he was reporting how he had spent most of one day in search of a new study lamp.

This was a man with an unusual interest in and eye for furniture, as well as for houses, which frequently, in his fiction, seem to have a personality of their own. In a very few words he can convey an immediate picture: 'a lame invalid of a sofa'; 'blind houses, with their eyes stoned out'; a bedroom 'fitted all about with lockers and drawers, was like a seedsman's shop'. He enjoys describing buildings: Bleak House was 'one of those delightfully irregular houses where you go up and down steps out of one room into another . . .' So searching for a house might have been an inconvenience from the point of view of his work, but not an unpleasant one.

Though he was becoming successful, money was scarce. He sought – and obtained – an advance of £100 from Richard Bentley, moved his family to lodge briefly in Marylebone at 30 Upper Norton Street (its name was changed to Bolsover Street in the 1870s) and made an unsuccessful offer for one unidentified house. Shortly afterwards, he found 48 Doughty Street, not far north of Gray's Inn. He was attracted to it because it was in a private road with a gateway at each end. On duty at each gate was a porter or beadle in a mulberry uniform and gold-laced hat. It wasn't long before a beadle had made his appearance in the book he was now writing in monthly instalments, as was to be his usual practice, *Oliver Twist*: here was where Mr Bumble was born.

Dickens agreed to take over the tenancy, for £80 a year, from the Reverend Joseph Banks, if he would first paint the front drawing room and frames round the windows, and the ceiling needed to be cleaned. In March he wrote to John Forster about the harassment of dealing with the 'crew (I know no better word for them) of house agents and attornies', causing him to almost miss his conveyance to Chalk and driving him 'more than half wild besides'. House purchasers will sympathize. By the end of the month, however, he was in his new home, though bewailing the 'worry and turmoil of "moving"'. In April he was still unravelling the problems, writing to Richard Bentley full of anxiety about the next issue of *Miscellany*, as all the upheavals associated with his

The hallway of 48 Doughty Street.

48 Doughty Street, now the Charles Dickens Museum.

RIGHT The drawing room at Doughty Street, restored to its appearance during Dickens's residence.

BELOW The bedroom of Mary Hogarth, Catherine's sister.

move 'have thrown me back so, that my time this month is more precious than ever'.

The house must have seemed hugely spacious after Furnival's Inn. It had two garrets on the top floor, in one of which Dickens's brother Fred probably slept, with the other one a nursery; on the second floor was the bedroom of Charles and Catherine, a dressing room, and 'a back room with cupboards' for Catherine's sister Mary. The drawing room was on the first floor at the front, with a small back room leading off, which would serve as Dickens's study. There was a toilet on the landing, but no bathroom.

The dining room was on the ground floor at the front, with a morning room at the back and a cloakroom leading into the garden. In the basement were the kitchens, washhouse with sink and copper, where water for the household was heated, coal and wine cellars. Behind the house was the mews; still cobbled, it is now called Brownlow Mews in honour of the benevolent old gentleman who looks after Oliver Twist.

So, by the age of twenty-five Dickens was running a twelve-roomed house and a household comprising a cook, a housemaid, a nurse and a groom. In *The Uncommercial Traveller*, published in 1861, he writes of the area as the 'certain distinguished metropolitan parish' and 'a house which then appeared to me a frightfully first-class Family Mansion, involving awful responsibilities'. His early letters written from this address, however, show his pleasure at being in his new home and organizing his growing household.

Within weeks this was shattered by the sudden and shocking death of Mary, still only seventeen. She died catastrophically suddenly of a heart attack after a joyful trip to the theatre. She 'expired' in his arms, he told almost everyone. 'Thank God she died in my arms,' he wrote to Thomas Beard. 'And the very last words she whispered were of me.' Dickens, ever the respecter of his own feelings, wrote many letters detailing his utter and increasing devastation: the loss was grievous; she was 'the grace and life of our home'; 'the dearest friend I ever had'. Naturally he

Mary Hogarth, who died at the age of seventeen, just weeks after the family moved into Doughty Street.

CHARLES DICKENS AT HOME

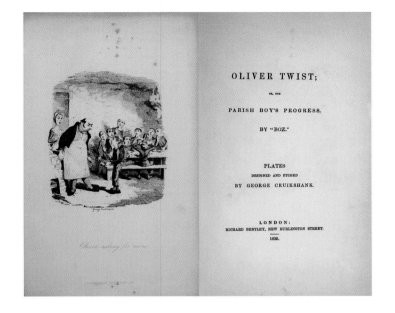

LEFT Collins's Farm (renamed Wyldes Farm), where Dickens took his family to recuperate after the loss of Mary Hogarth.

ABOVE Title page of *Oliver Twist*, which Dickens was writing at the time, alongside *The Pickwick Papers*.

had encountered deaths already, but this was the first that affected him so deeply, and perhaps permanently. He missed supplying his monthly episodes – of *The Pickwick Papers* and *Oliver Twist* – for the only time in his life. Mary remained always in Dickens's mind as an image of the perfection of womanhood. He wore her ring for the rest of his life, and she remained in the forefront of his mind as a precious memory: five years later, for example, he wrote to the American poet Henry Wadsworth Longfellow of her as 'my better Angel', and when staying at the Niagara Falls, pined for her – 'oh, that she had been there'.

Her death led to another change of scene: recuperation for him, and for Catherine, who suffered a miscarriage. They adjourned to Collins's Farm, a white weatherboarded farmhouse in a peaceful spot on the edge of Hampstead Heath, at what is now

the junction of Hampstead Way and Wildwood Road, near the – then – 'quiet little hamlet of North End': it was later renamed Wyldes Farm (recalling its fifteenth-century origins). He and his family remained there for a couple of weeks. 'We have come here for quiet and change. We have a cottage of our own, with large gardens, and everything else on a small and comfortable scale.'

Reinstated in Doughty Street, Dickens resumed his work. *Oliver Twist* was finished in early 1839. *Nicholas Nickleby* was already in train; he had started it on the eve of his twenty-sixth birthday and the first episode was published in March 1838. Each of them came out in monthly episodes in *Bentley's Miscellany*, which was where *Barnaby Rudge* – started in Doughty Street, but not completed there – was intended to appear, but he couldn't come to an agreement with Bentley. So he arranged with Chapman and Hall to produce a new publication, *Master Humphrey's Clock*, which was where it eventually appeared.

As the books came steadily, so did the children. Two more babies – Mary (usually called Mamie) and Catherine (always Katie, or Katey) – were born in 1838 and 1839. But despite the 'awful responsibilities' life continued to be convivial. He enjoyed meeting up with his friends: his letters and notes to friends are heavily sprinkled with plans for expeditions, invitations to ride or walk up to Hampstead Heath, and exhortations to 'come and have a chop'. 'You don't feel disposed, do you,' he wrote in January 1838 to John Forster, 'to muffle yourself up and start off with me for a good brisk walk over Hampstead Heath? I know a good 'ouse there [Jack Straw's Castle] where we can have a red-hot chop for dinner, and a glass of good wine.' Or, on another occasion: 'I am not well and want a ride. Will you join me say at 2 o'clock for a hard trot of three hours? Yes or No.' Or sometimes he just wanted to be sociable: 'Can you come and take a cutlet with us today at 5? Let me know and we'll add a bit of fish.'

Dickens threw as much energy into these endeavours as into his family. He was a sociable man; he belonged to the Garrick and

The Star and Garter hotel, scene of many celebratory gatherings for Dickens and his family and friends.

the Athenaeum. Along with the conviviality was the importance he placed on tradition and ritual – for example, for two decades from his second wedding anniversary onwards he and certain friends celebrated his wedding anniversary and Forster's birthday, which coincided, at the Star and Garter in Richmond. As Forster pointed out in his *Life*, 'it was part of his love of regularity and order . . . to place such friendly meetings as these under rules of habits and continuance'. The Star and Garter was an acknowledgedly grand hotel with terraced grounds overlooking the River Thames, described in a contemporary guide book as 'the renowned tavern and hotel, the "Star and Garter", more like a mansion of a nobleman than a receptacle for the public'. In an odd coincidence it burnt down the year that Dickens died.

That getting out of the house seems to have been as important to him as home and household is not surprising, given that he had a brood of children, and a host of relations, for whom he had

taken responsibility; one letter he wrote declined an invitation from the publisher William Longman: 'On Friday I have a family dinner at home – uncles, aunts, brothers, sisters and cousins – an annual gathering. By what fatality is it that you always ask me on the wrong day!' But the overall impression is one of contentment, of a man at ease with his domestic condition.

Henry Burnett, married to Dickens's older sister Fanny, gives a rare insight into one such evening at Doughty Street:

Mrs Charles Dickens, my wife, and myself were sitting round the fire, cosily enjoying a chat, when Dickens, for some purpose, came suddenly from his study into the room. 'What, you here!' he exclaimed, 'I'll bring down my work.' It was his monthly portion of Oliver Twist *. . . In a few minutes he returned, manuscript in hand, and while he was pleasantly discoursing, he employed himself in carrying to a corner of the room a little table, at which he seated himself and recommenced his writing. We at his bidding, went on talking 'our little nothings'; he every now and then (the feather of his pen still moving rapidly from side to side), put in a cheerful interlude.*

The house at Doughty Street, now a museum, gives an idea of the cosiness that this scene conjures up. Dickens's study leads off the drawing room, which, after a certain amount of detective work by curator David Parker and staff of the museum in 1983, was restored to a close approximation of how it was in his tenancy. The schedules of property attached to the tenancy agreement, before and after the Dickens family's residence there, indicate the changes made. Beforehand, the room had a dado and was papered above; afterwards the paper had been brought down to the skirting board, which was a much more fashionable style. Other changes in the schedules show that the fireplace was changed. Scrapings of the woodwork were taken to establish the 'knowable shade of pink' in which it is now painted.

At the time when the drawing room was refurbished it was decided to remodel the kitchen of the museum. The original kitchen of Dickens's time had for several years been kitted out as if in a scene from a *Pickwick Papers* Christmas. It was decided, 'without regret', as David Parker wrote in *The Dickensian*, to transform it into a library of works by and about Dickens, now used by researchers and for meetings.

Back in the 1830s, Dickens's library was not at this stage extensive. The essayist and critic G.H. Lewes recalled visiting the house and observing that Dickens had very few books, and those he had were undistinguished: 'nothing but three-volume novels and books of travel, all obviously the presentation copies from authors and publishers'. There were no 'treasures of the bookstall, each of which has its history, and all giving the collection its individual physiognomy. A man's library expresses much of his hidden life. I did not expect to find a bookworm, nor even a student, in the marvellous "Boz" but nevertheless this collection was a shock.' Lewes did then add that the man himself did much to make up for that: 'His sunny presence quickly dispelled all misgivings', though Lewes left 'more impressed with the fullness of life and energy than with any sense of distinction'.

In the hall of the museum is a display of more fact and fiction: fixed on the wall is 'A Genuine Dickens Relic', the window of the little attic in Bayham Street; and above is a window from Pyrcroft House, Chertsey, through which Oliver Twist is said to have been pushed by Bill Sikes on the occasion of the burglary.

It seems plain that Dickens took the lead in domestic decisions – the cash book for Doughty Street, for example, is in his handwriting, not Catherine's. And clearly these decisions were an aspect of life he enjoyed. His enthusiasm for home-making and attention to detail are illustrated by his discovery of a suitable house in Devon for his parents (his solution to the increasingly bothersome embarrassment of his father's constant running up of debts and trading in London on the Dickens name). In March

The library at the Charles Dickens Museum, converted from what was once the kitchen.

1839 he wrote to Catherine from the New London Inn in Exeter about 'a jewel of a place', Mile End Cottage in Alphington, a mile from Exeter, where his parents stayed until the end of 1842: 'I cannot tell you what spirits I have been put into by the cottage I have taken . . . Something guided me to it . . . It is on the road to Plymouth, in the most beautiful, cheerful, delicious, rural neighbourhood I was ever in.' There was 'an excellent parlor with an open beaufet [a recessed cupboard for china] in the wall and a capital closet, a beautiful little drawing-room above that.' There were cellars and safes and coalholes, as well as a 'noble garden'. All was 'exquisitely clean and the paint and paper from top to bottom are as bright as a new pin'. The rent (including taxes), he concluded exultantly, was only '£20 a year'.

Shortly afterwards, he wrote again to expand on the details of the furniture after his visit to the upholsterer who had originally provided it: the lesser sitting room would have six imitation rosewood chairs, drop-leaf table, Kidderminster carpet and some second-hand red curtains; the best sitting room would have better chairs, a sofa table, couch, white muslin curtains and Brussels carpet. The best bedroom, a tent bedstead (a bed with curtains) and white furniture; in the next a French bed (also curtained) with painted furniture. He had not neglected the necessary items for the kitchen, such as crockery and glass. And, eager to remove his parents from London as quickly as possible, 'there will be fires in all the rooms on Thursday morning'.

His mother was allowed back to London on occasion – for example, for Catherine's confinement and the birth of Katie in the autumn of 1839. Three years married and with three small children, the Dickens household required several servants – and a larger house. So Dickens embarked on house-hunting again. Or, at least, he deputed his mother to search. In November, he thought he had found one just south of Regent's Park, as he told Forster: 'a beautiful (and reasonable) house in Kent Terrace, where Macready once lived, but larger. Mother is going tomorrow to scrutinize, and I really think it'll do.' He wrote to his friend William Macready, the actor, for advice about the house: 'the terms seem promising . . . unless your recollection serves you with any decided objection to Kent Terrace itself which presents a just cause or impediment'.

Macready certainly did have an objection, which was swiftly conveyed. A few days later Dickens was writing to Thomas Mitton, his friend and solicitor, instructing him to withdraw the offer, as Macready had advised that 'the stench from the stables at certain periods of the wind was so great they could scarcely breathe'. He sent his mother off again on another house hunt: 'My mother is going to look at the house in Ulster Place and another one this morning, but I begin to droop and despair.'

So his mother had her uses. She had helped in other ways before – for example, when he had lived at Furnival's Inn, she had covered a sofa for him. But this bout of proxy house-hunting

came when he had been traducing her in *Nicholas Nickleby*, where she is regarded as being the original for the deficient mother Mrs Nickleby. Her part in his miserable service in the blacking factory – unknown to anyone else – still rankled.

Whether it was her doing or his – he spent some time searching himself – within two weeks he had found 1 Devonshire Terrace, opposite the York Gate entrance to Regent's Park on Marylebone Road. He wrote with enthusiasm to John Forster that 'a house of great promise (and great premium), "undeniable" situation and excessive splendour, is in view. Mitton is in treaty, and I am in ecstatic restlessness.' According to Forster, it was 'a handsome house with a garden of considerable size, shut out from the New Road by a high brick-wall facing the York Gate into Regent's Park'. With his characteristic alacrity he undertook to take it from 1 December, paying £800 for the residue of a fourteen-year lease dating from 20 March 1837. The rent was twice that of Doughty Street at £160 per year.

At the same time, he was diligently detaching himself from Doughty Street and in negotiation with the landlord. He was contracted to pay rent until March, but was hoping that a new tenant might come in at Christmas, and was extolling the virtues of the fittings, which, he emphasized, he had improved and added to, with new blinds fitted at every window and 'many little conveniences here and there'. He was also prepared to sell on the drawing-room carpets, fender and fire-irons, curtains and fitted cornices, and the oil cloth in the passages, all in excellent condition.

His efforts were successful. Then there was the agony of actually moving. 'Did you ever "move"?' Dickens wrote in a letter to the poet Samuel Rogers. 'We have taken a house near the Regents Park intending to occupy it between this and Christmas, and the consequent trials have already begun. There is an old proverb that three removes are as bad as a fire. I don't know how that may be, but I know that one is worse.' To another friend he grumbled: 'I

am in the agonies of house-letting, house-taking, title proving and disproving, premium paying, fixture valuing, and other ills too numerous to mention. If you have the heart of anything milder than a monster, you will pity me . . .'

He was also busy acquiring furniture, including dining-room chairs for £22 6s., and commissioning William Snoxell of Chancery Lane, decorator and window-blind-maker: 'Mr Charles Dickens will thank Mr Snoxell to send to a house to which he is on the point of removing, (No. 1 Devonshire Terrace, York Gate – close to Marylebone Church) and measure the dining-room windows for white sprung roller blinds. Between three and four today would suit well for the measuring, but if that is inconvenient to Mr Snoxell, he can send as early as he pleases on Monday.'

By 12 December 1839 he and his household were installed. In a letter to Mitton that day from his new home, he asked Mitton to name a time for execution of the lease at his office. Soon after

LEFT The keystone over the door of 1 Devonshire Terrace is now in the garden of the Charles Dickens Museum.

ABOVE Drawing by Frederic Kitton of 1 Devonshire Terrace, now demolished, where Dickens moved in 1839.

Christmas, he was excusing himself for the delay in writing to a contact, blaming his new home and all the necessary appointments with carpenters, bricklayers, upholsterers and painters.

The house, 1 Devonshire Terrace, no longer exists. It was demolished in 1957, though the keystone over the door, displaying a classical bearded face, is now in the garden at Doughty Street. There is also a reminder of its significance on the wall of the office block that replaced it: a carved relief that shows the head of Dickens and characters from the novels he wrote during his time there, with the label 'While living in a house on this site, Charles Dickens wrote six of his principal works, characters from which

Carved mural commemorating the books Dickens wrote while living at
1 Devonshire Terrace.

appear in this sculptured panel.' The characters are Jacob Marley appearing to Scrooge in the form of a door knocker in *A Christmas Carol*; Barnaby Rudge and his raven Grip; Little Nell and her grandfather from *The Old Curiosity Shop*; Paul Dombey and his daughter Florence from *Dombey and Son*; Sairey Gamp from *Martin Chuzzlewit*; and Mr Micawber with David Copperfield. It is a neat encapsulation of the amount of work that was done in the twelve years that he lived at Devonshire Terrace. And that was only the half of it.

Dickens's campaigning work began in earnest during this decade: he visited Ragged Schools and took up other social causes, but he was also involved in the fight to save Shakespeare's house in Stratford-upon-Avon, and began relentless battles over copyright. His household expanded: six children were born during his time in Devonshire Terrace and Catherine's sister Georgina arrived in 1842 – she was nearly sixteen – and became 'Aunt Georgie'.

Perhaps a turning point in his success was in 1843, the year he wrote *A Christmas Carol*: it sold 60,000 copies on Christmas Day, and is credited with changing people's attitudes to Christmas. It was the first of his series of Christmas books, and he became for ever associated with that festival – helped no doubt by the overtly jolly life he developed at this new large home.

The house was an end house in a terrace of three built in 1776. It had a rather grand arched doorcase of rusticated stone. There were thirteen rooms on two main floors plus basement – with its kitchen, butler's pantry, still rooms and cellars – and two attic storeys: the children's day and night nurseries were on the lower of these, and the servants' bedrooms on the upper. The house had handsome bay windows, and a wide garden, which – apparently – contained two WCs (there was also one on the first floor of the house) and a two-stall stable and coach house with groom's room above.

The drawing room and two best bedrooms were on the first floor. On the ground floor were the dining room and the library. We know, from an interview Dickens gave to a French journalist, Paul Forgues, in 1843, that he worked in the library, and that it was an 'oval room, simply furnished'. It also had an iron staircase to the garden. William R. Hughes, whose *A Week's Tramp in Dickensland* is an invaluable source, as he was writing within two decades of Dickens's death, wrote of how he met the decorator Benjamin Lillie, who did much work for Dickens there and in his later homes. Lillie described how Dickens would lie in the garden with a handkerchief over his face and then run inside to write a few sentences before resuming his position in the garden.

We have a good idea of what Devonshire Terrace looked like and how it was furnished from an inventory for the different rooms made out in May 1844, when Mrs Sophia Onslow, a widow, moved in for a year (for a rent of £300) when Charles Dickens took his family to live in Genoa. He had let the house before, when he and Catherine visited America in 1841, but there is no trace of an inventory then. This time there was a detailed

Georgina Hogarth, Catherine's younger sister,
who came to live with the family in 1842, in a painting by Augustus Egg.

Illustration by Dickens's artist friend John Leech of Mr Fezziwig's ball from
A Christmas Carol, written in 1843.

inventory, partly in Catherine's hand and partly in Charles's: it was probably compiled in a hurry, as Mrs Onslow wanted the house directly. Since their journey to Italy was not beginning until the start of July, they all had to decamp rather briskly to a house nearby in Osnaburgh Terrace.

One can tell from this inventory that the theme that Mary Hogarth had drawn attention to, in her brief description of Furnival's Inn – rosewood in the drawing room and mahogany in the dining room – was continued here. One can also sense the essential conviviality and hospitality of the household: the dining room contained twelve green leather-covered chairs, and the mahogany dining table had up to five additional leaves. There was a mahogany sideboard with a carved back, bought while Dickens was in Doughty Street, presumably in preparation for his move to the rather grander premises, and which is now back in Doughty Street again. Crimson damask curtains framed the window. There was a 'Turkey carpet' on top of fitted oilcloth – a common floor covering in those days. There were gilt lamps and a candelabra, light from which must have been brightly reflected in the gilt picture frames and wall mirrors of which Dickens was so fond. His daughter Mamie wrote that 'he had a passion for looking-glasses, so there were looking-glasses placed in every corner of the house'.

More evidence of the Dickens's hospitality is indicated by the itemization of the crockery: the best dinner service included

Charley, Dickens's eldest son.

pots – four silver shells containing sweets, and a silver filigree temple in the middle! But here the very candles rose each out an artificial rose! Good God!'

But Dickens's hospitality extended beyond dinners. A particular focus was at Christmas, New Year and Charley's birthday on 6 January, which from his earliest years was an excuse for Dickens to celebrate. There were dances, Scottish reels, plays (theatricals were becoming an important preoccupation for Dickens – he formed an amateur dramatics company in 1845) and conjuring. Jane Carlyle wrote in another much more admiring letter about Dickens's skill and the plum pudding trick:

Only think of that excellent Dickens playing the conjuror for one whole hour – the best conjuror I ever saw (and I have paid money to see several) – and Forster acting as his servant. This part of entertainment concluded with a plum pudding made out of raw flour, raw eggs – all the usual raw ingredients – boiled in a gentleman's hat – and tumbled out reeking – all in one minute before the eyes of the astonished children and the astonished grown people!

She also mentioned how he turned 'ladies pocket handkerchiefs into comfits . . . and a box full of bran into a box full of a live guinea-pig!'

Presumably this entertainment took place in the drawing room, though it's not clear how there was actually any space for guests. The 1844 inventory for the drawing room makes startling reading for the very quantity of its contents: apart from the fire screens and ornaments, of which there was a considerable number, the room held eight tables, a rosewood cottage piano (presumably brought from Furnival's Inn), a dozen chairs, two couches, two ottomans, two small high-backed praying chairs 'worked in embroidery' and a 'worked pedestal screen, and cover to match' (these were probably made by Catherine, as she did

54 dinner plates, 20 soup plates and 2 soup tureens. There were, of course, dessert services too – three of them – and another couple of dinner services: a blue one and 'a common Green dinner-set'. An insight into their entertaining can be gleaned from the rather sardonic letter of Jane Carlyle to a friend in 1849 about their way of serving: 'A dinner at Dickens' last Saturday where I never went before . . . The dinner was served up in the new fashion – not placed on the table at all – but handed round – only the dessert on the table and quantities of artificial flowers – but such an overloaded dessert! Pyramids of figs, raisins, oranges – ach!' She compared it to a dinner held by a friend of hers, an aristocratic hostess, Lady Ashburton: 'there were just four cowslips in china

much embroidery). There was a large mirror in a gilt frame over the chimney piece. These were the early days of Victorian England, and though Dickens preferred the Regency style, one is reminded of the comment of his contemporary and friend Wilkie Collins on a 'richly furnished' Victorian drawing room: 'the eye ached looking round it'.

The ground-floor library, which was Dickens's study, had four tables including a 'french polished mahogany revolving study table, with drawers', a table that travelled with him to his future houses and was clearly a favourite of his for its propensity for secreting keys. He was obsessive about security. When he commissioned Thomas Beard to go to his house on an errand, he instructed him to 'twist round the revolving table in the middle of the room, open all the drawers – there is alternately a real drawer and a sham, and the key is in one of them – until you find a half bound Diary.' Another letter home enclosing a key starts with instructions to 'open the drawer in the round table – take out the same bunch as before – find another key on it, that opens the corresponding table nearest to the drawing room'. In a later letter, the enclosed key was the key for his writing table: 'In the left hand-top drawer is a bunch of keys, one of which has a bone-label attached to it. That key is the key of the nest of drawers on the top of the stand with the looking-glass door, between the new window and the large window. In one of those drawers . . .' were two books!

The library by now, incidentally, held 2,000 books, all listed in this inventory; G.H. Lewes, on another visit to Dickens, was better pleased. While waiting in his library he 'of course glanced at his books. The well-known paper boards of the three-volume novel no longer vulgarized the place; a goodly array of standard works, well-bound, showed a more respectable and conventional ambition; but', he added critically, there was still 'no physiognomy in the collection'.

Mrs Gaskell dined at Devonshire Terrace and wrote to a friend about the house:

We were shown into Mr Dickens' study . . . It is the study where he writes all his works; and has a bow window. There are books all round, up to the ceiling, and down to the ground; a standing-desk at which he writes; and all manner of comfortable easy chairs. There were numbers of people in the room [these included the Carlyles, Forster and Hablot Browne, who illustrated Dickens's works] . . . *In the evening, quantities of other people came in. We were by this time up in the drawing-room, which is not nearly so pretty or so home-like as the study.*

She commented too on the 'nice little Dickens children in the room – who were so polite, and well-trained'.

Also itemized in the library were 'One Mahogany What Not and Writing Desk', a mahogany book stand, one rosewood letter box, a desk and candle sconce, a Brussels carpet, white curtains flanked by yellow silk damask curtains and 'a spring recumbent reading chair'. The compilation of this detailed inventory was just as well, perhaps, as Forster says that 'his house was let to not very careful people'. Dickens's letters from Genoa in the months before their return indicate a need for remedial action, which was an excuse for him to arrange extensive redecoration. ' ,' he wrote to Mitton in April 1845, 'will you set your man to work to paint the outside of the house? I should like all the doors and railings in the garden to be a nice bright cheerful green', all except the little staircase from the window, which he would prefer to remain white. He also wanted the hall and staircase painted 'a good green: not too decided, of course, to spoil the effect of the prints'.

Other paint schemes were specified. And, an important innovation, he wanted a letter box installed – with a glass back 'so that John [his manservant] may see when there are letters in the inside'. In this, Dickens was keeping up with the times. Rowland Hill had in 1837 drawn up plans to revolutionize the Penny Post, saying: 'There would not only be no stopping to collect the postage, but probably it would soon be unnecessary even to await the opening of the door, as every house might be provided with a letter box into which the Letter Carrier would drop the letters, and, having knocked, he would pass on as fast as he could walk.' By the 1840s letter boxes were becoming popular: Harriet Martineau, a visitor to Devonshire Terrace and later a contributor to *Household Words*, wrote to a friend, 'we are all putting our letter-boxes on our hall-doors with great glee'.

Then Dickens came to a project he had obviously been pondering on in his sojourn abroad, and for which he wished an estimate: 'I must know the expense . . . before I decide . . .' He wanted to 'new-paper' the drawing room, taking away the ugly hand rail and bringing the paper down to the skirting board.

> *I should like the skirting board to be painted in imitation of Satin-wood – the ceiling to have a faint pink blush in it – and a little wreath of flowers to be painted round the lamp. The paper must be blue and gold or purple and gold – to agree with the furniture and curtains; and I should wish it to be cheerful and gay . . . I have said nothing about this to Mrs D: wishing it to be a surprise, if I do it at all. Gold moulding round the paper.*

He may not have mentioned that to Catherine, but he certainly discussed the colour scheme for the hall with her, for on 20 May he wrote to Mitton: 'Kate thinks with you, that green for the hall and staircase is quite out of the question. I merely mentioned the color without much reflection, as one for which I have a natural partiality. So let it be whatever you and the Decorator think best – not so cold as to be dull, and not so warm as to suffocate the prints.' In the event, the estimate for the drawing-room decoration was 'what Mr Swiveller calls a staggerer [*The Old Curiosity Shop*]. I had no idea it would mount so high. It really should be done; for as it is, it is very poor and mean in comparison with the house – and I have been "going" to do it these five years.'

Along with the decorating instructions for Devonshire Terrace were the requests necessary after a long absence: for the gardener to put the garden in order, and to add a coat of gravel to the walks; for Snoxell to take down and clean the blinds; for the annual jobs of taking up the carpets – by Rudkin the carpenter – and the house to be cleaned from top to bottom, by Josephine, who was also employed once a year. But that was to be done only when workmen had finished. Dickens can be seen to be trying to work out the timetable from a distance, but even his fabled powers of organization were unable to prevent the state of mess still prevailing on his return from Italy.

It was not long after his return that he began his collaboration with the philanthropist Angela Burdett Coutts over the setting up of Urania Cottage, 'A Home for Fallen Women'. He had met her in the late 1830s, and she, recognizing his energy and direction, had enlisted his willing help in the administration of her charitable work, dealing with the many begging letters that she received, and in the initiation of schemes. When she wanted to build model homes, 'sanitary dwelling houses for the poor', he looked for suitable places, such as a slum called Hickman's Folly, in which he vividly describes the 'odious sheds for horses, and donkeys, and vagrants, and rubbish, in front of parlor windows – wooden houses like horrible old packing cases full of fever'. He pressed the case for flats, knowing from his own experience the misery of lodgings and sub-lettings, but also for practical reasons: 'They would have gas, water, drainage, and a variety of other humanizing things which you *can't* give them so well in little houses.' He also thought they would take up less space, allow people to live closer to work and would allow easier access to country walks.

Urania Cottage was to be their biggest joint enterprise. The idea for the home came from Miss Burdett Coutts in 1846 but was seized upon and developed by Dickens, and after discussion, he threw himself into it wholeheartedly. He found the house at Shepherd's Bush (which was later demolished to make the BBC's

Lime Grove studios, which in turn made way for, appropriately, social housing), then secluded and surrounded by gardens, and wrote 'An Appeal' for distribution to likely young women in police custody or coming out of prison: the emphasis was on 'HOME':

She has resolved to open . . . a place of refuge . . . and to make it a HOME for them. In this Home they will be taught all household work that would be useful to them in a home of their own and enable them to make it comfortable and happy . . . In this home, which stands in a pleasant country lane, and where each may have her little flower-garden if she pleases, they will be treated with the greatest kindness: will lead an active, cheerful, healthy life: will learn many things it is profitable and good to know; and being entirely removed from all who have knowledge of their past career, will begin life afresh, and be able to win a good name and character.

Not unnaturally, he had definite ideas on the regime: the women would rise at 6.00 a.m., and after morning prayers and breakfast, there would be school for two hours every morning. They would be taught to bake bread, do laundry and needlework. There would be improving texts on the walls. Many of the details about Urania House, which was operational for fifteen years, are in an article he later wrote, entitled 'Home for Homeless Women', published in *Household Words* in 1853. As was consistent with his interests, he took charge of organizing maintenance and choosing furniture and furnishings, even the material for the dresses for the inmates, communicating always with Miss Burdett Coutts, as in his letter of November 1847, just before it opened: 'I have laid in all the dresses and linen of every sort for the whole house – purchasing the materials at Shoolbred's in Tottenham Court Road, at the wholesale prices. I have made them as cheerful in appearance as they reasonably could be.'

The following summer he was telling her about his 'great council' with the blind-maker, who showed him 'such good

Angela Burdett Coutts, the philanthropist with whom Dickens collaborated on Urania Cottage, 'A Home for Fallen Women'.

John Forster, Dickens's lifelong friend and future biographer.

reasons for the common outside Venetian blinds, drawing up into cases, being at once the most enduring, the neatest, and cheapest, for our purpose, that I unhesitatingly concluded to order that kind'. He drew up specifications of work to be done for painting and repairing. He discussed the installation of gas: 'The gas is now at the gate. Would you like it taken into the house? The expense will be the usual fitting and nothing more.' If the principle was agreed, he recommended 'a jet in the fanlight at the entrance, in

kitchen, wash-house, bathroom and in each bedroom over the chimney piece. Then no light would ever be carried about the house. Just as we do here.'

He was endlessly practical. When Miss Burdett Coutts devised a scheme for helping the soldiers in the Crimean War – she wanted to install a machine for drying clothes, such as the one that was in Urania House – it was Dickens who found the man to make a larger one, and explained in comprehensible detail to Miss Burdett Coutts how it would work. He was involved in everything from the selection of residents and arbitrating on their fate to repairing the gate and planning an extension ('I know my plan is a good one – because it is mine!'). All this was organized around his normal – excessive – workload and his long absences.

In 1846, the year he began his seventh novel, *Dombey and Son*, Dickens became, at the age of thirty-three, editor of a national newspaper, the newly founded *Daily News*. He was in the position for eighteen days. He quickly decided that it was not the right role for him and Forster took over, but the fallout in terms of pursuit by former and would-be contributors stoked his wanderlust, and he decided to take his family abroad for a year, settling on Lausanne for six months, followed by Paris.

He was, however, anxious about his relinquished income and kept his name on the rolls at Middle Temple. He wrote to a friend: 'I am (nominally, God knows) a law student and have a certain number of "terms to keep" before I can be called to the Bar; and it would be as well for me to be called, as there are many little pickings to be got.'

He let Devonshire Terrace to Sir James Duke (MP for Boston, although in 1847 he was also Lord Mayor of London) but early the following year he was 'driven from post to pillar' in search of a house: Charley, by now a pupil at Eton, had scarlet fever, and had been discharged into the care of his maternal grandmother. Naturally the anxious parents wanted to be near him, and returned from Paris, leaving the rest of the children in charge of Catherine's sister Georgina, and eventually managed to secure 1 Chester Place until June. In fact, though they were close to the house where Charley was being looked after by Mrs Hogarth, they were not allowed to visit him, as Catherine was pregnant again and the doctor did not want her – or Dickens – going near Charley because of the possibility of infection. It was a difficult period for them: Dickens told one friend that he was 'living a Tartar kind of life, in a sort of Tent hard by'.

They did not get possession of Devonshire Terrace until August. By then they had ensconced themselves in Broadstairs for the summer break, but Dickens was making frequent visits to Devonshire Terrace, 'very anxious to get it thoroughly in order'. That year he was obviously planning other improvements but, discovering that his lease was two years shorter than he had supposed, he cancelled some building work for which he had received an estimate. One wonders if this might have been a conservatory, given his recurring desire for one over the years.

He was galled to find that he would be leaving Devonshire Terrace soon, as he had recently gone to the expense of having gaslight put into the hall, staircase and kitchen – expensive commitments for a rented house. Gas had been used in public buildings for some years – and he had first considered it in 1843 – but the problems of sooty ceilings had to be overcome before it could be considered for domestic use; and great care had to be taken, as can be seen in the instructions he gave to servants, about closing the hall doors when the gas was lit, and taking special care when the street door was open.

Partly, perhaps, because of this outlay, he determined not to rent again: in July 1850 he told Mitton, his friend and solicitor,

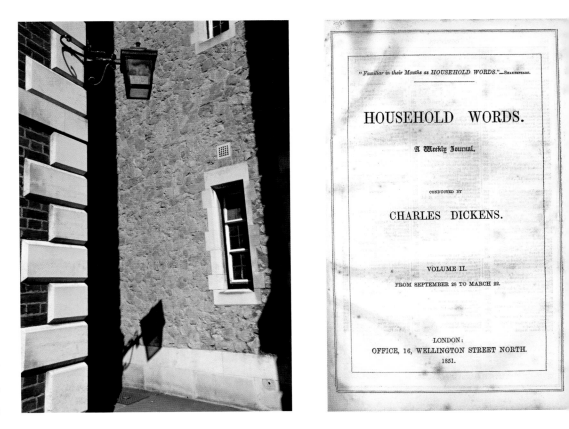

LEFT A corner of Middle Temple, where gas lighting is still used.

RIGHT Cover of *Household Words,* the journal Dickens launched in 1850.

that could he find any purchase to suit him, he would 'certainly not *rent* another house'.

By the end of the decade, he was house-hunting for another purpose: an office for his new journal, *Household Words*, eventually located in Wellington Street, Covent Garden. One advantage of his brief period at the *Daily News* had been his experience of working there with William Wills, who became the journal's sub-editor, and until almost the end of his life was an invaluable colleague and support. One thing Dickens had decided upon early was that the title page would carry the words 'Conducted by

Charles Dickens'. Choosing the title took a little longer, though when he had hit on *Household Words*, which he thought a very pretty name, all followed on swiftly.

The preliminary words for the first number on 30 March 1850 were: 'We aspire to live in the Household affections, and to be numbered among the household thoughts of our readers' and, in this and its successor, *All the Year Round*, there was a steady thread of articles of domestic interest, reflecting his own predilections, some of which he wrote, as well as on his campaigning preoccupations, such as sanitation in an article after a cholera outbreak calling for 'homes, instead of polluted dens', and the hearth in 'On the Chimney Piece'. He particularly favoured 'process' articles – accounts of manufacturing processes of plate glass or paper, for example. There were pieces on fish markets and banks, and the art of carving meat (at which Dickens was very skilled). Dickens and Wills wrote a piece on Staffordshire pottery and porcelain: 'A Plated Article'. And there is an extremely lengthy one on wallpaper, written by Dickens and called 'Household Scenery'. It starts off, 'Most people amuse themselves at one time or other of their lives, by fancying what sort of house they would like to live in', and devotes 6,000 words to wall coverings from tapestry to *gutta percha*, but mainly to wallpaper in more aspects than one could possibly have dreamed of, showing the interest that such subjects held for him. In the first six months he wrote nineteen pieces – while he was still writing *David Copperfield* – and read far more: in 1852 he estimated that he read 900 manuscripts for the journal.

There was one other endeavour in which he was undoubtedly involved while at Devonshire Terrace: a book, *What Shall We Have for Dinner? Satisfactorily Answered by Numerous Bills of Fare for from Two to Eighteen Persons* by Lady Maria Clutterbuck, actually Catherine Dickens. The name was taken from the part she had played in *Used Up,* one of Dickens's innumerable theatrical enterprises. Published in 1851, her book contains many suggestions with roasts, boiled salmon as well as cock-a-leekie,

hotchpotch, hashed hare, fried oysters, woodcocks, leg of mutton with oysters, stewed eels followed by raspberry jam sandwiches (but made of pastry), sweet omelettes, steamed puddings and an awful lot of toasted cheese at the end – though this is reduced in later editions. The care taken in and around this production, and the thought that has gone into the recipes, extraordinary though some of them seem these days, put into perspective Charles Dickens's later recorded disdain for Catherine as a domestic manager. For all his holding of the purse strings and his close involvement in household affairs, she must have been pretty organized, or at least flexible in adapting her schedules and household management – and menus, as there were continual moves from house to house or to temporary accommodation and holiday homes. But it is also likely that he was involved in this project, as well as writing the introduction. Any examination of his writings shows how much Dickens is interested in food: there is much variety and much detail, for example, in *Nicholas Nickleby* in Ruth Pinch's efforts at making a beefsteak pudding (later taken up by Eliza Acton), and stuffed mutton with oysters appears in *Little Dorrit* – apparently a favourite of Dickens. Interestingly, he disparages unseasonal food: 'I abhor the idea – whether it be for winter peaches, spring lamb, midsummer ice, unnatural cucumbers . . .'

Sometimes, though, he chafed at the bit of domesticity. In 1841 he wrote to a friend: 'Have you ever had two babies in the house at once? – of your own, I mean. Our third child can't walk yet, and here is a fourth on her heels. I am expecting every day to be gray and have very nearly persuaded myself that I am gouty.'

He was able to compartmentalize his life, but he was affectionate to his young brood, involving himself with his children, flinging himself into their games and anxious to make time for them. Once he asked Mitton to come early to dinner: he had been out every day that week and had scarcely seen the children. 'If we dine so late as 6, it is their bedtime when the cloth is removed – and I don't like to deprive them of the opportunity of coming down . . .'

But of course, he was equally devoted to his creations. His children noticed. His eldest son Charley remarked: 'I am certain that the children of my father's brain were much more real to him at times than we were.' His elder daughter, Mamie, wrote:

After a hard morning's work he was sometimes quite preoccupied when he came in to luncheon. Often he would come in, take something to eat in a mechanical way . . . and return to his study to finish the work he had left, scarcely having spoken a word in all this time. Our talking at these times did not seem to disturb him, though any sudden sound, as the dropping of a spoon or the clinking of a glass, would send a spasm of pain across his face.

Dickens himself wrote, as he ended *Oliver Twist*: 'I would fain linger yet with a few of those among whom I have so long moved.' One of the alterations made at Devonshire Terrace was to add an extra door to the study to protect him from noise.

Dickens's time at Devonshire Terrace spanned many sadnesses – the deaths of his elder sister, Fanny, of his father, and of a third daughter (Dora), aged only eight months – but the years here were very social, and, according to Forster, 'full of pleasant gatherings, when, besides the dinner, the musical enjoyment and dancing, as his children became able to take part in them, were incessant'.

One cannot help feeling that this was a happy house. Forster wrote: 'any special regard for houses he had lived in was not a thing noticeable in him. But he cared most for Devonshire Terrace, perhaps for the bit of ground attached to it; and it was with regret he suddenly discovered, at the close of 1847, that he should have to resign it "next Lady-Day three years. I had thought the lease two years more."'

It was time to start looking for another house.

Fanny, Dickens's elder sister, as portrayed in a drawing by Samuel Laurence.

DICKENS AWAY: IN BRITAIN

Dickens's adult life was characterized by movement. This energetic, ever-restless man needed to travel, to have a change of scene, to see new places. But he also hankered after home. Wherever he was, he was compelled to impose order in his environment, and to arrange the furniture to his satisfaction: an indication, perhaps, of a need for control in his adult life after a chaotic childhood. He needed to set up home in the different places he stayed in, however briefly, a habit he adhered to throughout his life. When staying in Folkestone in the 1850s he told Wilkie Collins 'I went out after dinner to buy some nails (you know the arrangements that would be then in progress)', by which he meant hanging pictures, part of his usual process of settling in.

He often remarked upon the way he rearranged furniture in rented houses or in hotels, and how he prepared for his day's work by aligning table and chairs in a precise position. In a letter to Forster from Broadstairs in 1840, he wrote: 'Before I tasted bit or drop yesterday, I set out my writing-table with extreme taste and

The beach at Broadstairs.

neatness, and improved the disposition of the furniture generally.' On arriving at a hotel on his trip to Scotland where they had neglected to book rooms they 'were obliged to make a sitting-room of our own bed-chamber; in which my genius for stowing furniture away was of the very greatest service'.

Dickens spent much of his time away from his main home. Most often, this was with his family, in summer homes taken for months at a time. There were also trips with friends or for research, for example with artist Hablot Knight Browne (whose illustratons appeared under the name Phiz) to Yorkshire in 1838 to research for *Nicholas Nickleby*. Motivated by the sort of reforming zeal that had lain behind *Oliver Twist*, and alerted by a law case the previous year, he wanted to investigate Cheap Schools. In an extraordinarily short time, considering the length of journeys in those days, they surveyed the scene, spending two days in Greta Bridge, Barnard Castle and Bowes. It was an effective expedition: within years the sort of Yorkshire schools he described had closed.

There were expeditions, energetic jaunts with friends . . . Forster fondly recalls a vigorous afternoon in 1848 riding on Salisbury Plain, and a much longer excursion to Cornwall in 1842 with

Daniel Maclise and Clarkson Stanfield. 'There were Railways by then,' wrote Forster in his *Life*, 'but not many; but where the roads were inaccessible to post-horses, we walked.'

There was always walking: the long walks with friends – for example, in East Anglia at the genesis of *David Copperfield*. And there was, of course, also solitary and single-minded walking, around the streets of London, around his beloved Kent, over the South Downs, once – when he was particularly disturbed in mind – from London to Rochester. He came to believe that it was as important to spend as much time walking as working, and no doubt he was actually doing both when walking.

And for a large part of his life he would make temporary homes away from London, places where he could settle down to work. But while he always wrote wherever he was staying, he was also always hospitable, combining work and pleasure. Early in his marriage, he and Catherine adjourned to Elm Cottage, in Petersham, a place they revisited later for four months in 1839. The idea was that, removed from the usual calls on his time, he would have time to write, but also for his family and friends. Forster recalls the sort of afternoons spent there in a house where

> *extensive garden-grounds admitted of much athletic competition from the more difficult forms of which I in general modestly retired, but where Dickens for the most part held his own against even such accomplished athletics as Maclise and Mr Beard. Bar-leaping, bowling and quoits were among the games carried on with the greatest ardour . . . Even the lighter recreations of battledore and bagatelles were pursued with relentless activity.*

There were other places that were within reach of his *locus operandi* in London: Collins's Farm, where the family went after Mary Hogarth died, for example. Then after Mamie's birth in March 1838, he and the family adjourned for the summer to Twickenham, to 4 Ailsa Park Villas, a house in big grounds

dominated at the front by fir trees, where there were boating trips. For several months in 1843, he rented Cobley's Farm: in March that year, he wrote to Beard that he had discovered 'a sequestered Farm House at Finchley, five miles and a half from the Regents Park, whereat I do beseech the honour of your company to dinner, next Sunday'. Finchley was then completely rural, with nearby hamlets such as Church End and Finchley Common. Dickens's Arcadian Retreat, as Forster termed it, was where he wrote *Martin Chuzzlewit* and where he devised Mrs Gamp on walks 'in the green lanes as the midsummer months were coming on'. A plaque on 70 Queen's Avenue, Finchley, marks the spot.

His removals with his family were usually for settled periods by the seaside or in a country village, though the trip to Scotland was hugely more adventurous, judging by his accounts of the wilds of Glencoe ('perfectly *terrible*'), a fantastically difficult journey across a river in which Dickens remarked on Catherine's bravery, and some curious hotels: 'The place was a mere knot of little outhouses, and in one of them were fifty highlanders *all drunk*.' It served – as so often his wilder experiences did – to fortify his belief in a quiet domestic life. In a letter in June to Forster regaling him with their hectic schedule in Scotland, Dickens added: 'The moral of all this is, that there is no place like home; and that I thank God most heartily for having given me a quiet spirit, and heart that won't hold many people. I sigh for Devonshire Terrace and Broadstairs, for battledore and shuttlecock . . . On Sunday evening the 17th of July I shall revisit my household gods, please heaven. I wish the day were here.'

For many years, Broadstairs in Kent was his 'home from home'. This fishing village had been made popular by the Duchess of Kent who, according to *The Illustrated Times* in 1857 and loyal to her nomenclature, 'visited it every summer for years, coming in with the strawberries and going out with the blackberries'. He had actually been considering Ramsgate but had then happened upon Broadstairs, stayed at the Albion Hotel and liked what he

saw. He described it as 'intensely quiet; built on a cliff whereon
– in the centre of a tiny semicircular bay – our house stands: the
sea rolling and splashing under the windows. Seven miles out are
the Goodwin Sands . . . whence floating lights perpetually blink
after dark, as if they were carrying on intrigues with the servants'.
The North Foreland lighthouse, 'a severe parsonic light', stared
grimly out to sea. 'Under the cliff are rare good sands, where all
the children assemble every morning and throw up impossible
fortifications, which the sea throws down again at high water.'

He took the family there for the first time in 1837, to lodgings

Broadstairs as depicted in an early nineteenth-century engraving by
Day and Haghe.

that had a parlour overlooking the main road: the shop on the
spot it occupied at 12 High Street has a plaque noting his stay
there. It is where he finished *The Pickwick Papers*. He returned, on
and off, for twenty years.

Dickens's next stay at Broadstairs, in 1839, was at 37 Albion
Street, a house near the Albion Hotel, 'where we had that merry
night two years ago', he wrote to Forster. The house had 'the most

Dickens's letter to the illustrator George Cruikshank about his completion of *Nicholas Nickleby*.

There was some initial domestic difficulty while the family was waiting for its cook to arrive. For the interim a woman had been recommended, but she got 'remarkably drunk . . . was removed by constables, lay down in front of the house and addressed the multitude for some hours'.

This was one year he kept a diary, of sorts. In fifteen days, twelve times the sole word adjoining the date was 'Work'. Subsequently, there were five entries of 'Sea Bathing'. That was after he had written the final number of *Nicholas Nickleby*, and then taken a steamer to London to correct the proofs.

The following year the family were in Broadstairs twice, during June at 40 Albion Street, next door to the Albion Hotel, a house they returned to in the two years following. Dickens was most cheerful here, he told his old friend Thomas Beard, 'because he started the old man and the child on their Curiosity-Shop wanderings from that mansion'. Characteristically, he had told Beard as he was writing *The Old Curiosity Shop* in 1840: 'the writing table is set forth with a neatness peculiar to your estimable friend, and the furniture in all the rooms has been entirely re-arranged by the same extraordinary character'.

Over twenty years later, in 1859, he returned to Broadstairs to visit his friend Wilkie Collins – feeling unwell, he had 'an instinctive feeling that nothing but Sea Air and Sea Water will set me right' – and found himself in the same place again. He had asked Collins to speak to the owner of the Albion Hotel, 'the Noble Ballard', to reserve a bedroom and 'quiet *writeable-in* sitting room . . . for his ancient friend and patron'. Shortly afterwards he was telling his daughters: 'I am now (Ballard having added to the hotel a house we lived in three years) in our old dining-room and sitting-room, and our old drawing-room as a bedroom.'

Broadstairs was very popular, as can be seen by a letter he wrote to Thomas Mitton when he was desperately trying to locate a holiday home for the following month: 'In short, nothing can be done without going down in person, for the place is very full

beautiful view of the sea from its bay windows that you can imagine. It is a *house* not a lodging.' He described the comfortable sitting room, large bedroom, nursery and other rooms, with 'kitchens etc in their usual places, entrances front and back, surprisingly clean beds, and a costively inconvenient water closet'.

The Albion Hotel in Broadstairs. For three years, the Dickens family stayed in a house next door, which was later incorporated into the hotel.

indeed, and the people wildly rapacious and rearing up on their hind legs for money. The day to go down upon is a *Monday*, for there is a chance of some family having gone out upon that morning, it being a great departure day.'

Fort House, according to Forster, was 'the residence he most desired there'. 'It stood prominently at the top of a breezy hill on the road to Kingsgate, with a cornfield between it and the sea.' He had, meanwhile, to be content with Lawn House, smaller but with the all-important sea views: and when Hans Christian Andersen visited in 1847, he described it as a 'narrow little house, but pretty and neat, the windows facing the Channel, the open sea rolling in almost underneath them'.

Eventually Dickens had his wish, and was able to rent Fort House. The first year, 1850, he was there until the end of October. He wrote to Catherine, whose arrival was delayed (she had just given

birth to their ninth child, Dora): 'The house is excellent. We were in mighty confusion last night and this morning getting it to rights, but it is now quite orderly and is full of sweet air, sea views and comfort.' He was soon even more enthusiastic: 'It is more delightful here than I can express – corn growing, larks singing, garden full of flowers, fresh air from the sea – O it is wonderful.' Fort House was renamed Bleak House by a later owner (for many years it had a small Dickens museum there, but now is a luxury bed-and-breakfast and events venue), and inevitably reality is blurred around its history, with assertions that this was the Bleak House of the novel – though that was set near St Albans and does not have anything overtly in common with Fort House – or that he wrote the novel there. In fact the novel he completed there, on 23 October 1850, was *David Copperfield*. It is probable, however, that the plot for *Bleak House* was gestating during his last stay in 1851: he began to write it in November of that year. It has been argued that the inspiration for the name might have derived from Dickens's impressions of Fort House, though that seems unlikely, as he called it 'the house of houses' many years later when Wilkie Collins stayed there.

An article written for *The Dickensian* in 1905 said: 'The best way of understanding Dickens' pleasure in the resort is to visit it – it still retains many of the features which rendered it so attractive to him.' And so it does today. It is very recognizable from Dickens's own description in an article he wrote for *Household Words* in 1851 entitled 'Our Watering Place'. One can still tick off the landmarks from it: Holy Trinity Church, 'a hideous temple of flint, like a great petrified haystack' (a little harsh); the 'excellent hotel' (now the Royal Albion, a Shepherd Neame establishment); the 'queer old wooden pier, fortunately without the slightest pretensions to architecture, and very picturesque in consequence'; the North Foreland lighthouse; and the 'fancy shops' with their 'capital collection': 'we are great in obsolete seals and in faded pin-cushions, and in rickety camp-stools . . . and in miniature vessels . . . and in objects made of shells that pretend not to be shells'.

Fort House, Dickens's favourite house in Broadstairs. It was later extended and renamed Bleak House.

CHARLES DICKENS AT HOME

There are changes, of course. The assembly rooms and attached library – so important to his seaside life – are now the Charles Dickens Inn. Bleak House has been extended in the crenellated style of the original building. The many places where Dickens stayed are all labelled by plaques – and a plaque on a house in York Street announces 'Charles Dickens did not live here'. Nor, despite the name, did he live at the Dickens House Museum on the seafront. But the inspiration for David Copperfield's aunt Betsey Trotwood did: Mary Pearson Strong's Tudor cottage (its location shifted to Dover in the book) was opened as a museum in 1973 with a recreation of Betsey Trotwood's parlour, down to the 'tall press' from which she took bottles to pour into the bedraggled David's mouth on his arrival there.

One of the best-known scenes in *David Copperfield* is Betsey Trotwood laying into the donkeys on the greensward in front of her house. There are no donkeys now, no greensward – though there is, in the spirit of the novel, a locked garden – but there were donkeys here in Dickens's time, as he says in 'Our Watering Place': 'Whenever you come here, and see harnessed donkeys eating clover out of barrows drawn completely across a narrow thoroughfare, you may be quite sure you are in our High Street.'

No sooner was Dickens installed in his various homes, and the furniture rearranged, than he would dispatch invitations to his friends – Mitton, Beard, Maclise, Forster – issuing instructions about catching the Ramsgate steamer from the wharf at London Bridge, telling them that the house was within a minute's walk of sea and baths, and urging them to join in the pleasures of Broadstairs. In one he wrote in 1840, 'come to the bower which is shaded for you in the one-pair front, where no chair or table has four legs of the same length, and where no drawers will open till you have pulled the pegs off, and then they keep open and won't shut again'. In another: 'The sea is rolling away, like nothing but the sea, in front of the house, and there are two pretty little spare bedrooms

The Betsey Trotwood parlour at the Dickens House Museum in Broadstairs.

waiting to be occupied.' In a third: 'The bathing machine beckons its wooden finger – and cocks its preposterous eye – on the sands.'

What friends remarked upon was that such seaside stays were also dominated by Dickens's relatives. It is not clear whether this was because the congenial Charles always invited people to stay or because the young master of the extended family felt compelled to take charge of his failing parents and therefore of his siblings too. Even while he was still in his twenties he was a paterfamilias for his own progeny and his parents' progeny as well.

For a long time Dickens loved Broadstairs and declared its virtues, quoting the tourist literature – 'as the Guide Book most justly observes, [it is] "unsurpassed for the salubrity and purity of the refreshing breezes which are wafted on the ocean's pinions from far distant climes"' – or simply enthusing lyrically. In August 1841 he wrote to Forster: 'The sun is sparkling on the water so that I can hardly bear to look at it. The tide is in, and the fishing-boats are dancing like mad. Upon the green-topped cliffs the corn is cut and piled in shocks; and thousands of butterflies are fluttering about, taking the bright little red flags at the mastheads for flowers, and panting with delight accordingly. [Here the Inimitable, unable to resist the brilliancy out of doors, breaketh off, rusheth to the machines, and plungeth into the sea. Returning, he proceedeth.]' It was a description that was echoed in an essay for *Household Words* ten years later: 'The boats are dancing on the bubbling water; the radiant sails are gliding past the shore, and shining on the far horizon; all the sea is sparkling, heaving, swelling up with life and beauty, this bright morning.'

There were other seaside homes – in Brighton, for example. He stayed in lodgings or at the Bedford Hotel – a Holiday Inn of rather less appealing architecture is now on the site – where he wrote some of *Dombey and Son*. His first stay at rooms in 148 King's Road was in 1847 for a couple of weeks in May, after he was attacked by a horse and needed to recuperate; and he returned in November 1848, and in March 1850 to write part of *David Copperfield*. But these were in the main retreats solely to write. 'I don't in the abstract approve of Brighton – I couldn't pass an autumn here: but it is a gay place for a week or so.'

He also stayed in Dover and Folkestone. In 1852 he was in Dover at 10 Camden Crescent, a pleasant bow-fronted house, for several weeks from the end of July to the beginning of October. Wilkie Collins stayed with him and described how breakfast would be at 8.10 a.m. precisely, after which Dickens would work until two o'clock; afternoons were for swimming and expeditions.

In later years he visited the Ship Hotel, later the Lord Warden Hotel (and now the Dover headquarters of Sealink). It was a place he took Catherine's sister Georgina when she was ill, and in 1864 he met Wilkie Collins there; naturally, he had a sitting room with a view of the sea. He defended it to Mary Boyle, a friend he had met through his acting, saying, 'You do scant justice to Dover. It is not quite a place to my taste, being too bandy (I mean musical, no reference to its legs) and infinitely too genteel. But the sea is very

148 King's Road, Brighton, where Dickens often stayed on visits.

fine and the walks are quite remarkable. There are two ways of going to Folkestone, both lovely and striking in the highest degree.'

Folkestone was desirable enough for him to write a piece on it for *Household Words*. The sea here had 'such movement in it, such changes of light upon the sails of ships and wake of steam-boats, such dazzling gleams of silver far out at sea, such fresh touches on the crisp wave-tops as they break and roll towards me'. He dubbed Folkestone 'Pavilionstone': 'And, if you want . . . to breathe sweet air which will send you to sleep at a moment's notice at any period of the day or night, or to disport yourself upon or in the sea, or to scamper about Kent, or to come out of town for the enjoyment of all or any of these pleasures, come to Pavilionstone.' In particular, he sang the praises of 'our great Pavilionstone Hotel' and of its landlord: 'Send for the good landlord and he is your friend.' The good landlord was so pleased ('in the Seventh Heaven of Delight') with the piece that he ordered five hundred copies of that issue.

Dickens stayed at 3 Albion Villas, a pleasant little house four doors from the church, on the cliff, in the autumn of 1855 when he was working on *Little Dorrit*, from mid-July to mid-October. He spent his time looking at the sea while he worked, he said, and climbing all the hills on the Downs when he had finished. There were some of the best walks he had ever taken: 'The Down-lands in this neighbourhood – principally consisting of a chain of grass-covered hills of considerable elevation – are enchantingly fresh and free.' He recounted how he, the Inimitable, 'having nothing particular to do – except a new book, twenty months long – *Household Words* – and sheer other trifles – has taken to expend his superfluous vitality in a swarming up the face of a gigantic and precipitous cliff in a lonely spot overhanging the wild sea-beach. He may be generally seen (in clear weather) from the British Channel, suspended in mid-air with his trousers very much torn, at fifty minutes past 3 P.M.'

There were many other places he visited, and many places claimed. He certainly visited Bath and Bristol to perform in plays. Whether he also stayed at the Hare and Hounds, a mellow stone coaching inn in 'Corsham yellow' at Pickwick in Corsham, as local legend has it, is more doubtful. But the claims of Winterbourne Country House (a hotel) at Bonchurch on the Isle of Wight are justified. Dickens made a reconnaissance visit there in 1849, and wrote to Catherine about it: 'cool, airy, private bathing, everything delicious. I think it is the prettiest place I ever saw in my life, at home or abroad. Anne may begin to dismantle Devonshire Terrace.' When the family arrived en masse, shortly afterwards, the novelist William Thackeray met them by chance on Ryde Pier, 'all looking abominably coarse, vulgar and happy'.

Dickens was soon writing to Beard, summoning him down as usual:

Behold my address . . . until end of September . . .
Inimitable B.
Winterbourne Villa,

Bonchurch,
Isle of Wight
! ! ! ! ! ! ! ! !
There is a Waterfall in the grounds which I have driven a
carpenter almost mad by changing into a
SHOWER BATH
– with a fall of 150 feet!

To begin with, Dickens enthused about everything: the views (only to be equalled by those of the Mediterranean); the variety of walks; the picnics with fires (at his express stipulation, along with an iron pot to boil potatoes in); the cheapness; the civility; the sea bathing; and the healthy coolness. But things deteriorated and he wrote to Forster a long letter about his debilitated state there: the healthy coolness had lost its charm. When their let was complete, the family retreated with some relief to Broadstairs, first to the Albion Hotel and then to the house next door, the one they had lived in for three summers. They were there until late October, and Dickens was happy: 'the air so brisk and bracing as it is nowhere but at Broadstairs – the Channel so busy and alive with shipping as it is nowhere but off Broadstairs – the hotel so cosey and like a private house as it is nowhere but in Broadstairs – everything as nothing is out of Broadstairs. Veeve la Broadstairs!'

But despite his relief then, he grew disenchanted in 1851: 'Vagrant music is getting to that height here, and is so impossible to be escaped from that I fear Broadstairs and I must part company in time to come.' He cited the miscreants – organs, fiddles, bells, glee-singers. 'There is a violin of the most torturing kind under the window now (time, ten in the morning) and an Italian box of music on the steps – both in full blast.'

And so he broke his long connection with the seaside town. It was for Dickens, at home and on holiday, a time of change.

A MAN OF MEANS: 1851–60

What enabled Dickens to manage his professional, home and holiday life was his flair for organization. A characteristic that was plain to all who knew him was his constant requirement for order. He needed to be settled to write, so a well-run house was vital to him. His sister-in-law Georgina Hogarth said everything with him went as by clockwork. When he set off back to England from his Genoa residence in 1844 – a long slow journey – to read his Christmas story *The Chimes* out loud to his friends, he exhorted Catherine to 'keep things in their places. I can't bear to picture them otherwise.'

He hated mess. 'Once more in my own house!' he exulted on returning home in 1845 before adding: 'if that can be called mine, which is such a heap of hideous confusion, and chaos of boxes'. There are references throughout his books to the importance of order: in *David Copperfield*, Agnes rearranging David's lodgings and Aunt Betsey cleaning her room (though a counter-balance is provided by the manic cleaning of Pip's sister in *Great Expectations*);

The Empty Chair, painted by Luke Fildes at Gad's Hill Place, shows some of the items that Dickens always kept on his desk wherever he was.

Esther Summerson, manager of *Bleak House*, the embodiment of household order, thrift and busyness that Dickens valued above all, who says self-deprecatingly: 'Every part of the house was in such order, and every one was so attentive to me, that I had no trouble with my two bunches of keys.' An article on Spitalfields in *Household Words* sums up his attitude: 'The intrinsic worth of every simple article of furniture or embellishment is enhanced a hundredfold (as it always may be) by neatness and order.'

A friend and fellow actor, Mary Cowden Clarke, once enquired, on observing the exquisite order and nicety of his study, if he did his everyday work there. His study was at the heart of his home. The general rule was that no servant was allowed into it, and the door was locked when he was not in it. As we have seen, he needed everything to be perfectly arranged. Each day he would position the items on his desk precisely: the blue ink and quill pens he always used, his paper knife, the calendar and the little ornaments that he acquired or were gifts. These included a cup ornamented with leaves in which fresh flowers were placed every day, a pair of bronze duelling toads, a rabbit on its haunches: all images 'for his eye to rest on in the intervals of actual writing', as his son-in-law

Charles Collins described them in an article for *Illustrated London News* after his death.

His writing desk and desk furniture travelled with him on his later reading tours, or were delivered to the houses he stayed in. Shortly after he arrived in Genoa in 1844, he wrote to Forster that the box from Osnaburgh Terrace had arrived at last and now he had his paper and ink stand and figures he could think 'with a business-like air of the Christmas book'. In Lausanne, two years later, he lamented that he could not start on *Dombey and Son* until the 'big box' arrived.

Marcus Stone, son of artist Frank Stone (an old friend of Dickens) and later an eminent artist in his own right, said of Dickens's home: 'The presiding influence of the master was visible all over the house, his love of order and fitness, his aversion to any neglect of attention, even in details which are frequently not considered at all. There was the place for everything and everything in its place.'

When Dickens visited Christiana Thompson, a young woman for whom he had felt a certain *tendresse* when he met her as Christiana Weller in Liverpool, he was horrified by the disorder in their home; he wrote disapprovingly to Catherine: 'I rather received an impression that . . . the household affairs went a little to the wall', commenting in particular on the two daughters that they were in 'a singularly untidy state – one (Heaven knows why) without stockings'. Their father, he noted, was teaching them in 'a disorderly old billiard room with all sorts of messes in it'.

Throughout his life, he never relaxed his extreme habits of tidiness. Wills, his faithful assistant at *Household Words*, noted that after their meal in the railway carriage en route to Liverpool to board a boat to America in 1867, he took out a clothes brush and swept up all the crumbs. In their recollections of him after his death, his children recalled the spot checks on their rooms, his high expectations in this regard and his reproofs. In her memoir, his elder daughter, Mamie, for all her partisanship (she was always loyal and very protective of his reputation), wrote

of how he would inspect the bedroom she and her sister Katie shared at Devonshire Terrace, 'a little garret room, at the very top of the house'. She put the most positive spin on it, recounting how he 'encouraged us in every possible way to make ourselves useful and adorn and beautify our rooms with our own hands, and to be ever tidy and neat', praising him for allowing them to put up 'unframed prints fastened with ordinary black or white pins'. But she also recalled that 'he made a point of visiting every room in the house once each morning, and if a chair was out of its place, or a blind not quite straight, or a crumb left on the floor, woe betide the offender'. He would even open their drawers to ascertain the neatness of their contents. If he did not like what he found, he would make a note and leave it – no doubt neatly folded – by their pincushion. Mamie accepted this tranquilly. Katie was a little more rebellious and would mutter, 'Oh what NOW?' on receiving the third 'pincushion note' in a week.

The obverse of this was the extraordinary care and interest he took over their new bedroom in Tavistock House, where they moved in 1851, when the girls were thirteen and twelve. Mamie described in an article for the *Cornhill Magazine*, after her father's death, how they were to be given 'a better bedroom than they had ever had before', which Dickens had promised the girls when they moved to the 'far larger and handsomer' house. It surpassed even their expectations. They found it furnished with love and thoughtful care, and with not a single thing in it, she asserted, that had not been expressly chosen for them, or planned, by their father. The wallpaper was patterned with wild flowers; the two little iron bedsteads were hung with a flowery chintz. There were two toilet tables, two work tables, two easy chairs – all, she thought, so pretty and elegant. When one considers that all this effort was taken in the days when bedrooms were not, as a rule, as luxurious as they are now, it was a singular achievement.

He was 'full of the kind of interest in a house which is commonly confined to women', Mamie recalled. 'He would

take as much pains about the hanging of a picture, the choosing of furniture, the superintending of any little improvement in the house as he would about the more serious business of his life.'

This is something that he conveys in his fiction. To take one novel, for example, in *Bleak House* the warmth and cosiness of real homes are set against the disorder of the Jellybys' home, the cold and 'comfortless rooms' of Chesney Wold – 'dreary and solemn the old house looks, with so many appliances of habitation, and

Sir Leicester and Lady Dedlock, with their solicitor Mr Tulkinghorn in their home in *Bleak House*.

with no inhabitants except the pictured forms upon the walls' – and the poverty of the brick-maker's house, 'one of a cluster of wretched hovels in a brickfield, with pigsties close to the broken windows'. The accolade given to Esther by Ada – 'you would make a home out of even this house' – is for a quality highly valued by Dickens.

Dickens's skills in the domestic arena were recognized, and his opinion obviously respected. From a letter to Miss Burdett Coutts in June 1854, shortly after he had dined with her, it seems that she had asked him for advice about a room in her house in Stratton Street, and his closing remarks indicated that he harboured 'a horrible desire to have the sole and entire direction of the furnishing of that wonderful little room'. A later letter refers wistfully to it again: 'I have been thinking of the furnishing of that room, and see it all in my mind's eye.'

When he got back from the family's summer residence in Boulogne that year, he tentatively asked whether the room had been done, and on being reassured, replied: 'I shall be delighted to convey my critical eye into the midst of it.' He arranged to visit on Wednesday 1 November, and wrote immediately afterwards from his office to tell her the result of his inspection. He had much to say: he approved of the fitted couches and writing table, but thought the general compactness of this important part of the room is 'greatly marred' by there being nothing in the piers on either side of the mirror opposite the door. 'It is quite clear to me that there ought to be in each of these narrow piers, a long tasteful piece of drapery, falling from the curtain-cornice as part of the curtains. It would hold the whole together, and make the rest tell for a great deal more than at present.' He was equally emphatic about the need for a table below the bookcase, because the bookcase was 'quite insanely perched in the air, without appearing to have any root in the ground – which is always disagreeable'. But more importantly '*there must be no table in the middle of the room*, or you destroy the fireside'.

He decreed no more than three chairs, grouped about the hearth: 'all the room will bear'. He noticed a pedestal for a bust and counselled against such an adornment. 'Lastly the Carpet is not at all in keeping. It should be something – of a small pattern of course – in dark chocolate or russet, with maybe a little green and red. The eye would rise from a dark warm ground, with

great pleasure, to the light walls and the rich-coloured damask.' He added finally and modestly, 'You will understand of course that I don't lay down these things as infallible Canons of Taste, but merely as things that my eye misses, and that I should think essential to completeness if the room were mine.'

In the same way as his delight in the house he found for his parents at Alphington nearly two decades before, this gives a striking insight into his profound interest and judgement in such matters. So for Dickens the chance to acquire and decorate a new house at the start of this decade was much more of a pleasing challenge than it would be for many. He started to look around in 1850, though by the end of the year he was writing to the estate agent William Phillips of Bond Street that he was thinking of letting his house for six months, in order to flee the Great Exhibition: he wished to avoid the many 'letters of introduction' he anticipated, a consequence of his increasing fame. He needed to leave space for developing a new novel, now that the last episode of *David Copperfield* had appeared (in November 1850), as well as for the effort involved in his new magazine, and all his other commitments such as the Royal Literary Fund, the Guild of Literature and Arts, Urania Cottage, and his usual speech making, campaigning on social issues and letter writing.

There were a number of false trails in his house-hunting. In January 1851, he was in touch with his invaluable brother-in-law Henry Austin about a house he had seen at Highgate. It was close to Holly Lodge, home of Miss Burdett Coutts, as he explained to her, along the private road (probably Holly Terrace) 'at the back of those obtrusive cottages, and is so well adapted to my young people that I have warily broken ground with the agents'. He told Austin with humorous horror of his visit and how the lady of the house 'with curls like tight sausages, rushed out, card in hand, and enquired of the humble individual who has now the honour to address you, if he were the real original inimitable to whom she was indebted for so many hours of – &c &c'.

But in March he informed Austin that he had lost the house. He had offered the asking price on the condition that the owners convey the freehold of a piece of land in front. But a competitor offered the same price without that stipulation. He lamented the missed opportunity, certain that he had made a mistake. Two days later, however, he had seen a house in Avenue Road, by Regent's Park and close to the canal, 'that is a decidedly good "Family Residence"', and requested Austin's advice about the building of a study. By the end of March he had made an offer for Balmoral House of £2,700 to William Booth, auctioneer and surveyor. His offer was not accepted – which was just as well: a few years later, apparently, a bargeload of gunpowder passing along Regent's Canal exploded opposite the house and wrecked it.

He was offered a house in Porchester Terrace, Bayswater, to rent but he resisted. He even seemed to be thinking of locating south of the river to Blackheath: in a letter to Catherine, he told her: 'I have sent Mamey and Katey with Georgina to Blackheath today, with powers to ride donkeys etc. I don't expect they will do much househunting, but I thought it would be a treat for the girls.'

Then in April his friend Frank Stone directed his attention to Tavistock House, where he was living: he was about to relinquish the lease and move next door but one. It was in a terrace, built between 1801 and 1805 by James Burton on the east side of Tavistock Square on two plots of land leased from the Duke of Bedford, and then divided into three: Tavistock House, Bedford House and Russell House, Stone's intended home. An iron fence with gates gave some seclusion; the drive leading into a front court with a carriage sweep and centre bed before the three houses lent distinction. Outside, we are told, there was a crossing sweeper called Alfred who was probably the inspiration for Jo in *Bleak House*. (The house was demolished in 1901 and the site is now occupied by the British Medical Association.)

In mid-July Dickens was writing to his trusted adviser, Austin, asking if he would visit Tavistock House, which was 'in the

Tavistock House, which Dickens bought in 1851.

dirtiest of all possible conditions', to give a surveyor's opinion on 'the likelihood of the roof tumbling into the kitchen, or the walls becoming a sort of bricks and mortar minced veal'. The house was cheap, commodious and, Dickens thought, 'might be made very handsome'.

Negotiations followed from Broadstairs, where Dickens was installed at Fort House for the summer months, about repairs to

Dickens in his study at
Tavistock House, in a
portrait by William Frith.

CHARLES DICKENS AT HOME

be done before the deal went through. His first offer was £1,300 ('which I make without any idea of bargaining for the property'), made the day after Austin's visit, because, despite the extensive alterations and decoration required, he thought it 'well suited to my purpose'. Shortly afterwards, he was discussing £1,450 and giving 'carte blanche' for up to £1,500. On 23 July he wrote jubilantly to Stone, the initiator, that agreement had been reached, and that he had instructed his solicitor, now William Loaden of 28 Bedford Place. The final figure was £1,542 in payment for the remainder of the lease (forty-five years).

By August he was anxious about getting on with renovations, and was suggesting to Stone that they 'swap' residences: Stone and his family could move to Devonshire Terrace. This would give Dickens the chance to get started with his plans for Tavistock House while he and his family were in Broadstairs. Marcus Stone recalled this 'excellent project' in his later memoir, and the Stone family 'emigrated to Devonshire Terrace as soon as possible and remained there a couple of months'. The drawing room there became Stone's studio. Marcus commented on the well-stocked library, 'the room in which *David Copperfield* had just been written', and gave an artist's-eye view on 'a charming little collection of pictures' in the dining room. These included characters from Dickens's books, portraits of himself and Catherine, watercolours by his friend George Cattermole, portraits and pencil drawings of the children and a Maclise picture of a waterfall from the Cornish excursion. In another example of the blurring between fiction and reality, Dickens had commissioned 'portraits' of Dolly Varden and Kate Nickleby by William Frith. 'These art treasures were arranged on the wall with great discrimination. The owner showed himself to be an excellent "hanger",' wrote Marcus approvingly. 'The same scheme of hanging was adopted in the new house and afterwards at Gad's Hill.'

Now that Tavistock House was empty, Dickens commissioned Henry Austin to oversee the works and, in his usual frenzy of activity, set about installing a servant to get things moving and organizing upholsterers: 'you know the regularity and precision with which the domestic affairs of a certain "Inimitable" creature are usually conducted'. But in early September he sent a panicky, though droll, letter to Henry Austin punctuated at intervals by the line – in caps – 'NO WORKMEN ON THE PREMISES'. 'Where are you?' he asked. 'When are you coming home? Where is the man who is to do the work?' He agitated about the rat that had appeared in the kitchen and the drastic work that needed to be done to the drains, before sweeping on with his revised ideas:

Going over the house again, I have materially altered the plans – abandoned conservatory and front balcony – decided to make Stone's painting room the drawing room (it is nearly six inches higher than the room below), to carry the entrance passage right though the house to a back door leading to the garden, and so reduce the once intended drawing room, now school-room, to a manageable size – making a door of communication between the new drawing room and the study . . . Curtains and carpets, on a scale of awful splendour and magnitude, are already in preparation, and still – still –

NO WORKMEN ON THE PREMISES.

But that same day he had a letter from Austin suggesting Cubitt, builder, of Gray's Inn Road, who, Austin thought, would have the alterations done within a month. The firm had been set up in 1810 by Thomas Cubitt, the leading master builder and one of the first to have a 'modern' system of employing all the trades under his own management – something that came in handy for Dickens. Dickens enthusiastically accepted Austin's suggestion, telling of the relief of 'Kate, who was in a great state of despair, but greatly recovered since the receipt of your note this morning, and begins to think that we *shall* have a house after all'. The work got under way at last – though at the start of October, when alterations were in full swing, he remarked on the 'delay of these lawyers! I'm not in legal possession of the house – haven't paid the Money – haven't signed anything.' (He finally paid in September the following year.)

There was much to do: to investigate the right of way of other occupants of the three villas, to plan the colour scheme, to arrange the transfer of shrubs which he had planted at Devonshire Terrace. His letter to Richard Wood, a nurseryman of Haverstock Hill, with its explicit and detailed warning to this new trader, gives an insight into the strict mentality of the author and householder: '*punctuality and dispatch* are conditions . . . which I always stipulate. I would on no account have anything done, near me or for me, that failed in these particulars. I attach such paramount importance to them that I think it indispensable to impress this upon you . . .'

From Broadstairs, Dickens fired off letters and demands in all directions: to Shoolbred's, the pre-eminent drapers and carpet warehouse in Tottenham Court Road (it remained throughout the century the place to shop for textiles for interior design); to carpenters William Smith, also of Tottenham Court Road, about repairing furniture and regilding mirrors and the exact positioning of glass in bookshelves in the drawing room; and to Austin, of course, full of practical details, as well as wild fancies, from his holiday home: 'I smell paint in the Sea . . . I dream that I am a carpenter, and can't partition off the hall.'

It's impossible to know how much Catherine was involved in Dickens's domestic decisions. No letters from her survive (Dickens destroyed all correspondence to him, saying that it was the only safe way of keeping it out of print). They had clearly discussed the colour scheme for Devonshire Terrace, and he was surely discussing the details of Tavistock House with her, and perhaps with Georgina, who had become very important in the household. But there is no doubt that he himself had strong views on almost everything, and involved himself in the minutiae of every domestic decision: the position of bells in the bedroom, the range in the kitchen, the dummy bookshelves. He wanted a sliding door, which would contain imitation backs of books, and he commissioned Thomas Eeles, bookbinder, to produce these. It is said that he might have been inspired by seeing something similar at Chatsworth when he had visited the Duke of Devonshire. But he visited Chatsworth – where he slept in a 'bedstead like a brocaded and golden Temple' – on 2 October, and by that time he had already sent to Austin 'a facetious list of letterings' for the backs of the dummy books. If they wanted fewer, he suggested that some of the sets be omitted, 'such as *Cats' Lives* in 9 volumes' (which wasn't, and is now at Gad's Hill Place).

One thing that particularly occupied his thoughts was the design of the bathroom. He wanted the WC partitioned off: 'the Bather would be happier and easier in mind, if the WC did not demonstrate itself obtrusively'; and later, appending what he called 'an elegant drawing', he indicated how he saw the 'light, cheerful-coloured waterproof curtains' hanging on a wooden frame, and emphasizing, 'What I want is, a Cold Shower of the best quality, always charged to an unlimited extent, so that I have but to pull the string, and take any shower of cold water I choose.'

By late October, he recognized with relief that 'faint streaks of civilization dawn in the water closet – the bath-room is gradually resolving itself from an abstract idea into a fact'. But this was tempered with despair: 'the drawing room encourages no hope whatever. Nor the Study . . . Catherine all over paint . . . Two men still clinking at the new stair rails. I think they must be learning a tune; I cannot make out any other object in their proceedings.'

At the same time he was, of course, dealing with *Household Words*, sorting out the serialization of *Cranford* by Mrs Gaskell, commissioning articles and writing some. He still had time to cram in a couple of theatrical performances in Bath and Bristol. And to give progress reports to his friends, like Thomas Beard: 'We have all manner of workmen, scooping, grooving, chiseling, sawing, planing, dabbing, puttying, clinking, hammering, and going up ladders apparently with no earthly object but that of staying there until dinner time, every day.'

By this stage the family was installed in Tavistock House and getting increasingly frustrated by the slow pace of proceedings (though modern observers might marvel at the apparent speed). Dickens communicated his feelings to Richard Watson on 31 October. 'I am perfectly wild to get into my new Study (having a new book on my mind [*Bleak House*]); and all the Trades of the civilised earth seem to be whistling in it, and intending to grow grey in it . . . We sit in our new house all day, trying to touch the hearts of the workmen by our melancholy looks.'

By the middle of November he was writing the first letters to be headed 'Tavistock House, Tavistock Square' – 'I am beginning to find my papers and to know where my pen and ink is' – though several of them were to complain about the water supply in his shower: the Waterworks Inspector had decreed that the cistern was too small and a new cistern was to be made.

It was all costing a great deal of money. The final bill for alterations was £577 15s. 6d. A letter to his publisher asked for money owed to be paid into Coutts Bank, adding dourly: 'It won't be there long.' In a letter to Austin on the same day he said: 'The figures are rather stunning – but it is a life business (I hope) and ought to be complete.'

In fact, as it turned out, it was not. But Tavistock House was, indeed, a domestic paragon, a show house. Visitors commented on the 'bright elegant interiors'. Hans Christian Andersen on his visit in 1857 described how in the passage 'from street to garden hung pictures and engravings. Here stood a marble bust of Dickens, so like him, so youthful, so handsome . . . ' Marcus Stone wrote: 'All the order and completeness of Devonshire Terrace was established on a more important scale. There was much new furnishing, my father's studio had become a green damask drawing room. This was on the first floor at the back looking onto the garden. The front

Marble bust of Charles Dickens, sculpted by Henry Dexter in 1842 on Dickens's visit to America.

room was his study or library in which a door of communication with the drawing room was masked by a sham set of bookshelves.' He noted that there was the same arrangement of pictures on the walls – though, of course, with more space, remarking approvingly: 'The whole establishment though sumptuously appointed was entirely without any suggestion of ostentation.'

Dickens (second from left) performing in *The Frozen Deep*, written by Wilkie Collins.

This was not George Eliot's view: after her visit to the house, she remarked rather cuttingly on the 'splendid library, of course, with soft carpet, couches etc, such as became a sympathiser with the suffering classes. How can we sufficiently pity the needy unless we know fully the blessings of the plenty?'

For Dickens, Tavistock House was a work in progress. Two years later when he was away in Italy on an expedition with Wilkie Collins and Augustus Egg, he was still thinking of plans for his home: he wrote to Catherine from Venice that he had been turning over in his mind 'an improvement in the study, which I wish you would have completed at once', bidding her to get an estimate from Shoolbred's. It was, in fact, a decorative embellishment – a fringed velvet covering for the mantelpiece, and in green, the colour of which he was apparently so fond: 'about the colour of the green leather to the bookcase, or a trifle darker if necessary. The green should be of a tint that will carry through both the bookcase green and the carpet green – generally – so that all the

greens tone in.' He was very precise – he wanted the sage–green fringe to be intermingled with red, and to echo the shape of the curtains' cornice fringe. A week later he was wondering if this study mantelpiece would be done by his homecoming; 'I hope so.'

There were, inevitably, certain problems later – the water in the shower continued to cause trouble and there was the need for a new 'modern dining-room stove', perhaps a Register stove, which he mentions elsewhere, which had an adjustable plate to control the flow of warm air to a room. Most important of all, for a man who loved his entertaining, was the need to strengthen the schoolroom floor: in September 1852, there were more instructions to Austin to relay to Cubitt about this project ('I don't care how many pillars they put in the Kitchen, so that the floor be made soundly and undeniably dance-proof'), along with a suggested remedy for dealing with water that collected outside the back door in wet weather, and a grumble that will resonate with all who have dealt with builders: '*That* slate has never been quite right since Cubitt's people left the roof.'

The reinforcements clearly were satisfactory because a grand dance was held that year. Mary Boyle remembered evenings

devoted to musicals and theatricals, and dancing in the New Year: Tavistock House . . . The very sound of the name is replete to me with memories of innumerable evenings passed in the most congenial and delightful intercourse; dinners, where the guests vied with each other in brilliant conversation . . . It seemed like a page out of A Christmas Carol, *as far, at least, as fun and frolic went: authors, actors, friends from near and far, formed the avenues of two long English country dances, in one of which I had the honour of going up and down the middle, almost 'interminably' as it seemed, with Charles Dickens for my partner.*

And there was the Tavistock House Theatre, set up in the schoolroom for a performance of Fielding's *Tom Thumb* for a

Twelfth Night party of 1854, with most of Dickens's children drafted in to perform and an audience of up to ninety. That was followed the next year by *Fortunio and his Seven Gifted Servants*, in which Dickens played Baron Dunover, and his son Edward, not yet three, was billed as Plornish Maroontigoonter Lightfoot, 'so small that he could hardly stand in the little top-boots which were made for him', Mamie recalled.

By 1856, much grander plans were afoot for a temporary extension to be built out from the schoolroom for the more ambitious *The Frozen Deep*, written by Wilkie Collins, though clearly with much input from Dickens. Preparations began early – in October the schoolroom was already in the hands of carpenters – and it cost £50 to put on, an astonishing sum for such a project. There were constant letters instructing scene painters; one to William Telbin asked 'what colored drugget would you prefer on the ground in the chamber? Red (which always tells), or green, or brown? The furniture being showy, I think the drugget should have no pattern on it.' The house was permeated with the preparations: 'All day long, a labourer heats size over the fire in a great crucible. We eat it, drink it, breathe it, and smell it.'

The play was an immense success. Dickens had thrown himself into the production from writing, through scenery, stage management and actual acting – he played the main role of Richard Wardour. It was inevitable that when it was all over, resulting in 'a mere chaos of scaffolding, ladders, beams, canvases, paint pots, sawdust, artificial snow, gas-pipes, and ghastliness', that he felt 'shipwrecked'.

With Christmas festivities, theatricals and holidays away, domestic life during this time had been apparently continuing on its normal course. The Dickens who was writing to Miss Burdett Coutts in May 1853 after her sister had had a baby boy sounded like the playful Dickens of old. Referring to Edward (later always called Plorn), who had been born in 1852, he wrote: 'I think that must be all a mistake about that Suffolk baby your nephew,

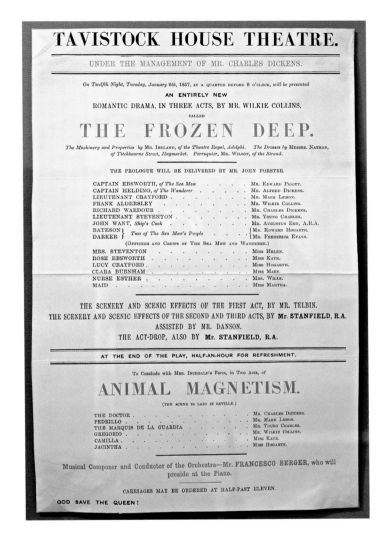

The theatre bill for *The Frozen Deep*, staged in January 1857.

because (it is a remarkable fact) we have in this house the only baby worth mentioning; and there cannot possibly be another baby anywhere, to come into competition with him. I happen to know this, and would like it to be generally understood.'

His letters to Catherine around this time were still affectionate. But there were undercurrents of discontent that were becoming more obvious. During the winter of 1855–6, when the Dickens family was wintering in Paris, Tavistock House was let to the Hogarths (Catherine's family), and he stayed there, or at the office of *Household Words*, in his sorties from Paris on writing business. In April when leaving Paris he determined to stay in Dover at the Ship Hotel, 'as the Hogarths don't leave Tavistock House 'till Saturday and . . . I cannot bear the contemplation of that family at breakfast any more'. He had already felt it necessary to remonstrate with them about their untidiness, as he told Catherine, and after their departure there was much reorganization and tidying to do. He transferred a dinner to the *Household Words* office after 'contemplating my dismantled study, with the carpet in the corner like an immense roly-poly pudding, and all the chairs upside down as if they had turned over like birds, and died with their legs in the air'.

But his humour was less evident when he wrote to Catherine: 'We have made a very different place of that establishment, by clearing out the dust on the first floor, where it lay an inch thick. We have swept and washed the Study and Drawing Room, opened the windows, aired the carpets, and purified every room from the roof to the hall. I have barely got to work yet, on *Little Dorrit*.'

His irritation with her parents and the explicit criticism must have weighed heavily on her, but perhaps this was all an outer sign of his deeper dissatisfaction. It was a vulnerable time for him. Just after his forty-third birthday, he had received a letter out of the blue from his first love Maria Beadnell, now Mrs Winter, which brought back vividly the emotions of his youth, the years when he had been so passionately in love. There was a briefly intense and intimate exchange of letters, though his subsequent meeting with her was deeply disappointing, and she was later satirized as Flora Finching in *Little Dorrit*. But the memories of his youthful passion had stirred him and clearly aroused feelings of unhappiness and put him into a state of restlessness.

Another factor contributing to his turbulent mood was his discovery on his birthday – which made it more portentous –

Maria Winter, formerly Maria Beadnell, Dickens's first love, who contacted him again in 1855.

that Gad's Hill Place, the house that was sanctified by precious memories of walks with his father, was for sale. He felt compelled to buy it, intending it as a holiday home. Poignantly, the first family celebration there was Catherine's birthday in May 1856. But then came the death of his friend the dramatist Douglas Jerrold, and Dickens in his usual generous and energetic manner – but

The Dickens Dramatic Company. Charles Dickens reclining at the front.

W.TELBIN · EVANS SHIRLEY BROOKS Mr LEMON Jun W.JONES F EVANS MARCUS STONE F.BERGER MARK LEMON Aug.EGG .
ALBERT SMITH Co.STANFIELD MISS EVANS · PIGOTT Mrs FRANCIS · LUARD
· KEITH CHAS DICKENS Jun KATE.DICKENS MISS HOGARTH MARY DICKENS WILKIE COLLINS MISS H.HOGARTH
CHARLES DICKENS

also anxious to work off his continuing restlessness – determined to reprise the production of *The Frozen Deep* as a way of raising money to look after his dependants. Not content with the fairly intimate stagings in London, in which his family played parts, he determined on a performance at the Manchester Free Trade Hall. This larger space was beyond the capabilities, he thought, of his womenfolk. He was introduced to the acting family of the Ternans, who lived in Islington: mother and three daughters, Fanny, Maria and Ellen.

The emotional experience of playing Richard Wardour in Manchester was stunning for both Dickens and, apparently, for Maria Ternan, who was so affected by his performance that the tears she shed in her role as she cradled the dying hero were genuine. The play must have engendered powerful emotions in this unsettled man, whose feelings were already jangled by memories of an early intense love. In the cast was the young Ellen,

the same age as his younger daughter but also barely older than Mary Hogarth, whose death had so profoundly distressed him. When he later discovered that Ellen had been born at Rochester, close to his own childhood home in Chatham, at the home of her uncle, a prosperous barge-owner, Dickens, with his belief in fate, must have seen this as a sign, another bond.

The conjunction of all these events plunged him into a strange state of extreme agitation. Not many months later he took off with Wilkie Collins on a journalistic expedition – to write 'A Lazy Tour of Two Idle Apprentices' for publication in *Household Words* – round the north of England, which happened to culminate in a week in Doncaster during Race Week, where the Ternans were performing. Though his arrival appeared to be random, Dickens's booking at the Angel Hotel had been made well in advance of his trip.

Just as he had involved himself in other people's lives, organizing and assisting them out of difficulties, so he now

The Ternan sisters – Maria, Ellen and Fanny – who took part in the Manchester performance of *The Frozen Deep*.

70 Gloucester Crescent, the house where Catherine lived after the breakdown of the marriage.

involved himself with the Ternans, urging them and helping them to move from their 'unwholesome' home at Park Cottage in Northampton Park. But this did not appear to be from his usual altruistic motives – and certainly Catherine would not have seen it as such. In October that year an irrevocable step was taken when he issued directions for the doorway between Catherine's bedroom and his dressing room at Tavistock House to be sealed up.

The following year, three days after her forty-third birthday, Catherine left the matrimonial home for 70 Gloucester Crescent,

north of Regent's Park. Only Charley went with her; the eight other children, between six and twenty, and her sister Georgina stayed with Dickens, and moved to Gad's Hill. The fallout from the separation was long and painful, and included a squabble with his publisher (Frederick Evans, who, along with a friend and editor of *Punch*, Mark Lemon, was representing Catherine's interests). With his certainty that he was in the right, and harnessing his usual energy, he divested himself of *Household Words*, and his publishers, and opened *All the Year Round* just up the road at 26 Wellington Street, agreeing a lease of twenty-one years at £110

a year from Stephen Bird, brick-maker of Kensington High Street. (The Charles Dickens Coffee House now occupies the premises.)

Miss Burdett Coutts tried hard to engineer a reconciliation, but Dickens was adamant – and though he remained in touch with her for the rest of his life, not least because his faithful sub-editor Wills also served as her confidential secretary, the familiar camaraderie and collegiate working were less evident. Urania Cottage, in which Dickens had become less involved, finally closed in 1862.

He flung himself into a frantic round of activity, after giving another public reading in aid of the Great Ormond Street Children's Hospital. He had given his first, of *A Christmas Carol*, for the Birmingham Industrial and Literary Institute, at Birmingham Town Hall at Christmas a few years before, and had found he enjoyed it. Now he considered it a commercial proposition and in April 1858 he gave his first paid public reading. By the following

year he had embarked on the tours that took up the rest of his life. The first was from August to mid-November 1859: 80 readings in 40 towns. The public performances provided a way of burning up the energy that he had thrown into his play-acting, and of assuaging his terrible restlessness.

'My father was like a madman when my mother left home,' Katie said later of this turbulent period, which 'brought out all that was worst – all that was weakest in him'.

For the next couple of years, he alternated between Tavistock House and Gad's Hill Place. When he finally sold Tavistock House and moved entirely to Gad's Hill Place in 1860, he made a big bonfire of all letters to him. It was a symbolic act. Despite the love and care that had been lavished on Tavistock House, it perhaps was never a homely dwelling: it was a place for theatre.

Dickens Away: Abroad

From the early 1840s Dickens had been spreading his wings. In 1842, he spent six months in America with the purpose of writing a book, accompanied by Catherine and her maid Anne Brown. Letting Devonshire Terrace to General Sir John Wilson, and leaving their four children at 25 Osnaburgh Street in the care of his brother Fred and his old friends, the Macreadys, who lived nearby, they set off from Liverpool in January. His description to Maclise of his cabin gives his impressions – none too complimentary:

I don't know what to compare it with. A small box at a coffee room is much too big. So is a hackney coach . . . It is more like one of those cabs where you get in at the back; but I think you could put on a shirt in one of those: and you certainly couldn't in this chamber. There are two horse-hair seats in it, fixed to the wall – one opposite the other. Either would serve for a kettle holder. The beds (one above the other of course) might both be sent to you per post, with one additional stamp. The pillows are

The medieval roofs of Boulogne, a favourite French resort of Dickens.

no thicker than crumpets; and the sheets and blankets are too ridiculous to write of.

For a man used to being able to order his environment this inflicted confinement must have been a profound shock. Indeed John Forster added in a letter sent to Maclise at the same time: 'What he has omitted was the indescribably comic shadow of momentary bafflement and discomfiture that came over his face when he first saw it.' What enabled him to recover so quickly, Forster pointed out, was 'Mrs D's cheerfulness about the whole thing. Never saw anything better. She deserves to be what you know she is so emphatically called – the Beloved.' There is markedly more enthusiasm here for Catherine than in his biography.

Dickens's arrival in America surpassed all expectation. His reputation had preceded him, and there was no time anywhere to relax, to pay attention to his surroundings, to set up home, as he was hustled from town to town. Unable to settle anywhere, deluged with invitations, besieged on all sides by fans eager to meet or even just to catch a glimpse of him, he found the trip hard going. Interestingly Catherine, who was initially reluctant to go, was the one who weathered all the inconveniences with grace and humour: Charles wrote of her with respect and approval. In a letter to Forster in April referring jokily to Catherine's propensity for falling and scraping herself, he nevertheless commended her as 'a *most admirable* traveller in every respect . . . [she has] never given way to despondency or fatigue, though we have now been traveling incessantly, through a very rough country, for more than a month, and have been at times, as you may readily suppose, most thoroughly tired; has always accommodated herself, well and cheerfully, to everything . . . and proved herself perfectly game'.

Though he was elated – as well as sometimes irritated – by the attention, he was desperately homesick. He bought an accordion and wrote to Forster: 'You can't think with what feeling I play *Home Sweet Home* every night.' The first letters from home did not arrive until mid-March, on an evening when Dickens was out at dinner. Catherine sent a note to him and, as Dickens recounted later, 'she didn't open them – which I consider heroic – until I came home'. They read them until nearly two in the morning.

Despite his fastidious nature he was also remarkably robust – how else could he have put up with the canal boat journey in March from Baltimore to Pittsburgh? He had to fish water out of the canal to wash his face, and slept 'on a temporary shelf exactly the width of this sheet of paper when it's open (*I measured it this morning*), with one man above me and another, below; and, in all, eight and twenty in a low cabin, which you can't stand upright in with your hat on.'

He described the inn in Pennsylvania as a rough log-house:

We had the queerest sleeping-room, with two doors, one opposite the other; both opening directly on the wild black country, and neither having any lock or bolt. The effect of these opposite doors was, that one was always blowing the other open: an ingenuity in the art of building, which I don't remember to have met with before. You should have seen me, in my shirt, blockading them

with portmanteaux, and desperately endeavouring to make the room tidy!

At the end of their travels, they were rewarded with ten days in May at the Niagara Falls. Letters dispatched headed 'Niagara Falls (upon the English Side)', underlined several times, described their quarters at the Clifton House Hotel and their view:

Our sitting room (which is large and low, like a nursery) is on the second floor and is so close to the Falls that the windows are always wet and dim with spray. Two bedrooms open out of it; one our own; one Anne's . . . From the three chambers you can see the Falls rolling and tumbling, and roaring and leaping all day long – with bright rainbows making fiery arches, down a hundred feet below us. When the sun is on them they shine and glow like molten gold.

Niagara Falls, a sight that enchanted Charles and Catherine.

But they both 'long ardently' for Devonshire Terrace. 'As the time draws nearer we get FEVERED with anxiety for home.' A letter to Forster on 26 May ends: 'Oh home – home – home – home – home – home – HOME!!!!!!!!!!!' In *American Notes*, published soon after his return, Dickens describes his eagerness on his journey home to be back at 'Heaven's fallen sister – Home'. These longings must still have been in his mind when he wrote *Martin Chuzzlewit*, based partly in America and published the following year, in which he writes: 'But it was home. And though home is a name, a word, it is a strong one; stronger than magician ever spoke, or spirit ever answered to, in strongest conjuration.'

But all the same, once back, he found it difficult to settle down. The trip had fired him with a sort of wanderlust and by March the following year he had made up his mind to 'see the world and I mean to decamp, bag and baggage, next midsummer for a twelvemonth'. He was to live abroad, on and off, for three years, and made frequent visits across the Channel for most of the rest of his life.

He settled on Italy, and both he and Catherine took Italian lessons in preparation. He first thought was that a favourable spot would be Nice, at that point in Italy. He toyed with Pisa, which he described as 'the Devonshire Terrace of my adoption', but then settled on Genoa. His friend Angus Fletcher – who had organized the Scottish trip – now lived there and Dickens wrote ebulliently to him, setting out his request for a house and the size required:

Here is a list of the Caravan
(1) The Inimitable Boz
(2) The other half ditto.
(3) The sister of ditto ditto.
(4) Four babies, ranging from two years and a half old to seven and a half.
(5) Three women servants, commanded by Anne of Broadstairs.

Genoa, home for the Dickens family for a year from 1844 to 1845.

Their first house was in Albaro, just outside the city walls. He had hoped to rent Lord Byron's home there, but it had fallen into neglect and become 'a third-rate wineshop'. Angus Fletcher found him Villa Bagnerello (so named for the butcher to whom it belonged) just up the road from Byron's house. It was 'unpicturesque and uninteresting', said Forster. It was originally called Villa di Bella Vista – and it certainly had that, overlooking vineyards and the bay. But Dickens himself dubbed it the 'pink jail'. 'It is the most perfectly lonely, rusty, stagnant old staggerer of a domain that you can possibly imagine.' It was bare, with little furniture, very clean, but 'the stable is so full of "vermin and swarmers" . . ., that I always expect to see the carriage going out bodily, with legions of industrious fleas harnessed to and drawing it off, on their own account'. Despite that, he proudly sent a sketch to John Forster, in which he explained exactly which rooms each of the fourteen windows visible referred to: 'The fifth and sixth, or two right-hand windows, sir, admit the light to the inimitable's (and uxor's) chamber. The bowery-looking place stretching out upon the left is the terrace, which opens out from a French window in the drawing-room . . .'

The villa still stands, in Via San Nazaro, and is now called Villa Barabino. A plaque was put up over the door in 1894: '*In questa villa dal primo prisco rosso delle sue mura Pink Jail ebbe gradita dimora Carlo Dickens geniale e profondo rivelatore del sentimento moderno*' (In this faded red villa, within its pink jail walls, Charles Dickens lived contentedly, a gifted and profound observer of modern sentiment).

Within a month he was planning to move to Palazzo Peschiere in Genoa (known thus because of its fishponds). During those few weeks, though, he found much to enthuse about in his new home: watching the lizards running up and down the walls; strolling along the narrow lanes; admiring the frescoes, painted on all the houses: 'Sometimes, I can make out a Virgin with a mildewed glory round her head . . . There are two old fresco-painted vases outside my own gate, one on either hand, which are so faint, that I never saw them till last night; and only then, because I was looking over the wall, after a lizard, who had come upon me while I was smoking a cigar above, and crawled over one of these embellishments in his retreat.'

There was also the appeal of the blue waters of the bay beneath. There were no bathing machines here, and he wrote gleefully to his friend Clarkson Stanfield: 'What do you think of my suddenly finding myself a swimmer? But I have really made the discovery; and skim about a little blue bay just below the town here, like a fish in high spirits.' And there were the sunsets: he wrote to Maclise, a painter: 'When the sun sets clearly, then, by Heaven, it is majestic! From any one of eleven windows here; or from a terrace, overgrown with grapes; you may behold the broad sea; villas, houses, mountains, forts; strewn with rose leaves – strewn with them? Steeped in them! Dyed, through and through and through. For a moment. No more.'

However, the appeal of Palazzo Peschiere – lauded in guide books for its position on the hill of Monte Bartolomeo, views out to sea and mountains, and terrace gardens with grottoes, statues, and orange and lemon groves – was far greater. There were goldfish swimming in the fountains; and the walks were marked out by hedges of pink roses 'which blush and shine through the green trees and vines, close up to the balconies of these windows. No custom can impair, and no description enhance, the beauty of the scene.' The palazzo had Corinthian plinths supporting a balustrade with alcoves occupied by draped figures. In front was a fountain surrounded by symmetrical flower beds divided by walks. It was far grander than any other house Dickens ever lived in.

And then there was the interior. He wrote to friends excitedly describing its *sala*, 50 feet high with frescoes three hundred years old, 'as fresh as if the colours had been laid on yesterday'. Right and left of the *sala* were the two best bedrooms, 'in size and shape like those at Windsor-castle but greatly higher'. Both had altars, a range of three windows with stone balconies, floors tessellated in patterns of black and white stone, and walls 'painted every inch, on the left nymphs pursued by satyrs as large as life and as wicked; on the right, Phaeton larger than life, with horses . . . tumbling headlong into the best bed'. One of these rooms served as Dickens's study, where he wrote behind a huge screen placed by one of the windows, from which he could see over the city – 'a wild medley of roof upon roof, church upon church, terrace upon terrace, wall upon wall, tower upon tower' – and as far as the lighthouse in the harbour.

It was at this 'enchanted palace in an eastern story', referred to in 'The Haunted Man', one of his Christmas stories, that the family had a magnificent Twelfth Night celebration, with a splendid cake that Miss Burdett Coutts sent out for Charley's birthday. There were splendid occasions 'when we enact grotesque charades, or disperse in the wildest exaggeration of an obsolete

country-dance through the five-and-twenty empty rooms'. Here Dickens dreamed again of Mary Hogarth.

As one might expect, he did not stay put. There were expeditions to Rome for Holy Week, and a dramatic and dangerous expedition to the very lip of Mount Vesuvius (with Catherine, Georgina, plus six saddle horses, armed guard and twenty-two guides). And just before Christmas 1844 he made the long and cold journey back to London with his courier, Louis Roche, to read his new Christmas book, *The Chimes*, to friends at Forster's house in Lincoln's Inn Fields (which he chose for the lawyer Tulkinghorn's residence in *Bleak House*).

The coach journey described in *Pictures from Italy*, published the following year, was in a world of flashing lights, half-sleep, drowsy meditation on the move. The writer Angus Wilson points out the particular significance of this journey as he was going from 'home' – (children, wife, his homestead in Genoa) to 'home' (London, friends, talk of his book, accolades). At home in Genoa, he had tranquillity in which to work, but there was

LEFT The Lincoln's Inn home of John Forster.

ABOVE A sketch by Daniel Maclise of Dickens's reading of *The Chimes* to friends at Forster's home.

also the absence of stimulating conversation, which he needed for his work. In London, there was the semi-public (even with friends) Dickens, with much banter, gossip and serious talk – and appreciation of his talents. In attendance at Forster's home were his brother Fred, Douglas Jerrold, Thomas Carlyle, Daniel Maclise and William Macready. 'If you had seen Macready last night, undisguisedly sobbing and crying on the sofa as I read,' he wrote jubilantly afterwards, 'you would have felt (as I did) what a thing it is to have power.'

The Dickens family returned home in the summer of 1845, but it was not long before he was contemplating another stay abroad, eager to leave the complications of editing the *Daily News* behind him. In April 1846, he was writing to the letting agent William

PICTURES FROM ITALY.

BY

CHARLES DICKENS.

The Vignette Illustrations on Wood by Samuel Palmer.

The Street of the Tombs: Pompeii.

LONDON:
PUBLISHED FOR THE AUTHOR,
BY BRADBURY & EVANS, WHITEFRIARS.
MDCCCXLVI.

Title page of *Pictures from Italy*, published in 1845.

Phillips of his intentions, and drawing attention to the fact that the halls and staircases of Devonshire Terrace had been repainted and the drawing room 'very prettily decorated'. The house was let for a year and the family set off for Lausanne in order to acquire, he said, some 'Mountain Knowledge' – which did not come in handy until *Little Dorrit*.

At Lausanne, he threw himself into house-hunting with his usual verve, discarding some houses because they were 'like small villas in Regents Park', with verandahs and glass doors leading on to lawns, and then at the other extreme a mansion in commanding position overlooking the lake but in a position that was too windy. Then he went back to the first house he had looked at: Rosemont: 'quite a doll's house', with two pretty salons and 'just enough bedrooms upstairs to leave the family one to spare'. It was on a hill (no longer – it was pulled down in 1938), overlooking Lake Geneva. There was a pavilion in the garden with two rooms and 'bowers for reading and smoking' scattered about the grounds, 'as in Chalk-farm tea-gardens'. The cost was to be £10 a month for half a year, and would reduce to £8 for the second half if he stayed.

It was furnished, though scantily, 'as all here are, though better than others . . . on account of its having been built and fitted up by the landlady and her husband for themselves who lived now in a smaller house like a porter's lodge, just within the gate'. His study looked out, through two French windows opening into a balcony, on the lake and mountains, 'and there are roses enough to smother the whole establishment of the *Daily News*'. Under the balcony was a stone colonnade, on to which the six French windows of the drawing room opened, and 'quantities of plants are clustered about the pillars and seats, very prettily . . . one of these drawing-rooms is furnished (like a French hotel) with red velvet, and the other with green; in both, plenty of mirrors and nice white muslin curtains', he wrote to Forster, then going on to describe every room in detail.

He was industrious here – he started *Dombey and Son* in June – though inevitably the English community issued many invitations. It was here that he made new friends: William de Cerjat, and Richard and Lavinia Watson, whose home was Rockingham Castle: Dickens described it to Forster after he had visited the Watsons there as 'a large old castle, approached by an ancient keep, portcullis etc etc, filled with company, waited on by six-and-twenty servants; the slops (and wine glasses) continually being emptied; and my clothes (with myself in them) always being carried off to all sorts of places'. *Used Up*, with Catherine as Lady Clutterbuck, was staged at Rockingham Castle in early 1851. He went there quite often until the death of Richard in 1852, the year when *Bleak House* first appeared, in which the castle posed as Chesney Wold:

> . . . *the old stone balustrades and parapets, and wide flights of shallow steps, were seamed by time and weather; and how the trained moss and ivy grew about them, and how the old stone pedestal of the sundial; and I heard the fountain falling. Then the way went by long lines of dark windows diversified by turreted towers and porches, of eccentric shapes, where old stone lions and grotesque monsters bristled outside dens of shadow and snarled at the evening gloom over the escutcheons they held in their grip . . .*

Dickens was taken by Lausanne, though he found it a little dull. There was one particular attraction: 'I never saw so many booksellers shops crammed within the same space, as in the steep up-and-down-streets of Lausanne.' And there was pleasant walking country, with vineyards, green lanes, cornfields and pastures full of hay. But he missed more urban streets: 'The absence of any accessible streets continues to worry me, now that I have so much to do,' he lamented to Forster, as he yearned for London.

At the end of the six-month initial let, the family packed up and adjourned to Paris. Dickens had seen the city briefly en route to Genoa and had been hugely impressed. Their first stop was at the Hotel Brighton. 'No man enjoyed brief residence in a hotel more than Dickens', said Forster in his *Life*, but 'several tons of luggage and other tons of servants' could not make this work, so he went house-hunting, which was 'frightfully severe'. He eventually found 'the most preposterous house in the world' at 48 rue de Courcelles in Faubourg St Honoré, with bedrooms like 'opera boxes'. He headed one letter 'At the Parisian Phenomenon', and to his new friend Richard Watson he described the dining room as 'a sort of cavern, painted (ceiling and all) to represent a grove, with unaccountable bits of looking-glass sticking in among the branches of the trees'. He added that 'there is a gleam of reason in the drawing-room. But it is approached through a series of small chambers, like the joints in a telescope, which are hung with inscrutable drapery.' To Forster, he added a PS: 'One room is a tent. Another room is a grove. Another room is a scene at the Victoria. The upstairs rooms are like fanlights over street-doors. The nurseries – but no, no, no more!'

It was an exceptionally cold winter – water froze in jugs and then burst them 'with reports like small cannon', and he was finding living very expensive, 'Fuel, stupendously so. In airing the house we burnt five pounds' worth of firewood in one week!' He was also finding it difficult to write. The fourth number of *Dombey and Son* was due, but he was distracted. He didn't like the room he had chosen for his study, so went to the drawing room. Even his usual rearranging the furniture didn't help. He said he 'went about and about it, and dodged at it, like a bird with a lump of sugar'. He finally got to grips with the number, writing to Miss Burdett Coutts: 'Paul [Dombey] is dead. He died on Friday about 10 o'clock, and as I had no hope of getting to sleep afterwards, I went out, and walked about Paris until breakfast-time.'

He came to like Paris very much, rather favouring it over London and enjoying the recognition he received in 'the dear old France of my affections', as he termed it in 'Travelling Abroad' for *All the Year Round*.

Victor Hugo's house in Paris.

He returned in the autumn of 1855 to search for another place for the winter. He found one at 40 Avenue des Champs-Elysées, but felt it necessary to lay the ground carefully to Catherine: 'you must be prepared for a regular continental abode'. There was only one window in each room, he said, but the windows looked on to the main street, where they would be able to see the 'wonderful life perpetually flowing by'. There were lots of

rooms, not especially well furnished, 'but by changing furniture from rooms we don't care for, to rooms we *do* care for, we shall be able to make them comfortable and presentable'. He described these rooms elsewhere as conjuror's boxes and meat safes. He also relayed to Wills that it required some firm action to get the apartment cleaned and newly carpeted, but it did have 'a really slap-up Kitchen near the stars!'

Characteristically, when he went to Victor Hugo's house, he was more interested in describing the furnishings – the old armour and tapestries – than their conversation. He likened Hugo's house to 'an old curiosity shop, or the property-room of some gloomy, vast, old theatre'. His dinner with Emile de Giradin, a writer and politician – and very rich – was notable for

three gorgeous drawing-rooms with ten thousand wax candles in golden sconces, terminating in a dining-room of unprecedented magnificence with two enormous transparent plate-glass doors in it, looking (across an antechamber full of clean plates) straight into the kitchen, with the cooks in their white paper caps dishing the dinner . . . The dinner done, Oriental flowers in vases of golden cobweb are placed upon the board.

Dickens revisited Paris often during the rest of his life, usually staying in hotels – his favourite was the Hotel du Helder, which, he told Mamie, was better than any he had put up in before – though he returned to an apartment at 27 rue du Faubourg St-Honoré in 1862 when Georgina was ill: a pretty apartment 'but house rent is awful to mention'. (This was at a time when Baron Haussmann was remodelling Paris and rents were rocketing.)

Later, for *All the Year Round*, he described the end of a railway journey to Paris: 'The crowds in the streets, the lights in the shops and balconies, the elegance, variety and beauty of their decorations, the number of theatres, the brilliant cafés with their windows thrown up high and their vivacious groups at little tables on the pavement, the light and glitter of the houses turned as it were inside out, soon convince me that it is no dream; that I am in Paris.'

The other place he became very attached to was Boulogne: there were family holidays there in 1853, 1854 and 1856, and much more discreet rendezvous there in later years, with Ellen Ternan. He had liked Boulogne – 'as quaint, picturesque, good a place as I know' he wrote in 1852 – and had determined to return: 'The best mixture of town and country (with sea air into the bargain) I ever saw; everything cheap, everything good; and please God, I shall be walking on those said ramparts next July.' He was, and he finished *Bleak House* in Boulogne.

Boulogne was a favourite resort for the English, and Dickens showed why in an article he wrote for *Household Words*, 'Our French Watering Place'. It was an old walled town on the top of a hill, and he commented on its 'houses with grave courtyards, its queer by-corners, and its many-windowed streets, white and quiet in the sunlight'. The walk on the old walls 'arched and shaded by trees' was 'made more agreeable and peculiar by some of the solemn houses that are rooted in the deep street below, bursting into a fresher existence a-top, and having door and windows, and even gardens, on these ramparts'. He described the 'little decayed market' which seemed 'to slip through the old gateway, like water, and go rippling down the hill to mingle with the murmuring market in the lower town'.

In Boulogne Dickens was the tenant of Ferdinand Beaucourt, a former linen-draper and town councillor who had built two country houses to let furnished on his hillside estate. The family's first home there was the Château des Moulineaux on rue Beaupaire, with comforts of all sorts 'beginning with no end of the coldest water . . . to English footbaths and a Parisian Liqueur-stand'. There were thirty-eight steps to the front door, and a quantity of buildings and features in the grounds, including a pavilion in the garden 'with a delicious view' for Wilkie Collins to work in when he stayed. There were 'five great summer houses, and (I think)

Sketch from the *Illustrated London News* of the Dickens family arriving in Boulogne.

fifteen fountains – not one of which (according to the invariable French custom) ever plays'. The plan of the property in the hall, Dickens commented, made it look 'about the size of Ireland; and to every one of the extraordinary objects there is a reference with some portentous name' – these included the Cottage of Tom Thumb, the Bridge of Jena, the Hermitage.

Curiously, he described the château as 'a charming doll's country house' (Dickens seemed to interchange doll's house, cottage and château, the last two 'to him convertible terms', according to Forster). Perhaps it was the size of the bedrooms that prompted him to describe it thus: 'eight tiny bed-rooms all opening on one great room in the roof, originally intended for a billiard-room'.

Pleasingly, there was much glass, and a 'perfectly beautiful' conservatory: he described to Forster the 'very pretty hall, almost all glass' and the conservatory had, he said, a comparable arrangement to that at Chatsworth, with a glass window in a mirror frame looking into it, just like the room of head gardener Joseph Paxton at Chatsworth, and opening on to a great bank of roses.

The chalet in Condette, rented by Dickens and lived in by Ellen Ternan and her mother.

The following year, they rented the second of M. Beaucourt's holiday homes, on top of the hill and overlooking a military camp where soldiers were preparing for the Crimean War. Dickens seemed equally enthusiastic about this house, though he described it to one correspondent as 'a regular triumph of French domestic architecture – being all doors and windows. Every window blows every door open, and all the lighter articles of dress and furniture fly away to all points of the compass. A favorite shirt of mine went to Paris (as I judge from the course it took) this morning.'

There's an indication of the huge organization involved with a household totalling twelve. They even took a horse and carriage with their coachman, Benjamin Cooper, from England. Dickens described how he saw the horse swinging from its harness during the course of disembarkation, and when writing to Miss Burdett

Coutts in 1854 he mentioned the arrival of his children and entourage after dark, 'with 27 packages, whereof 5 prodigious chests belonged to Mamey and Katy's governess, who is a Frenchwoman, and so small that I should have thought a hat box might have contained her entire wardrobe'. This letter also shows that he had not lost his habit of reorganizing houses, as he adds an aside about the 'variety of ingenious devices in the Robinson Crusoe way, effected by the undersigned (who I think has moved every article of furniture in the house, since Monday afternoon) which must be *studied* to be appreciated'.

He had just finished his tenth novel, *Hard Times*, as he told Collins: 'Bobbing up Corkwise, from a sea of Hard Times, I beg to report this Tenement – AMAZING!!! Range of view and air, most free and delightful – hill-side garden, delicious – field, stupendous.'

The aftermath of the rail disaster at Staplehurst, when Dickens tended injured passengers, as illustrated in the *Penny Illustrated Paper*.

The sojourn of 1856 was his last at Boulogne *en famille*, at Château des Moulineaux. Beaucourt had thinned the trees and planted the garden with flowers for each month they were to be there, including 'sweet peas nearly seven feet high, and their blossoms rustle in the sun like Peacock's tails'. The boys had their own little cottage in the garden, and Dickens devised a 'code of laws'; they took turns to be keeper for the week, Dickens apparently inspecting three times a day. But the holiday was curtailed suddenly because of an outbreak of diphtheria near by. M. Beaucourt was heartbroken at the ruin of his flower planting plans.

But it gradually emerged that it was not the end of Dickens's association with Boulogne or with M. Beaucourt, as he later rented a chalet from him at nearby Condette. Percy Fitzgerald visited it in 1902 after a chance discovery of '*La Maison Dickens*' made by Francis

Burnard, editor of *Punch*: it was 'beautifully situated with lovely views and a courtyard overshadowed by a big tree in the centre'.

Dickens visited Condette regularly from 1862 to 1865, when Ellen lived there with her mother. There are no charming descriptions of it: Dickens's letters, usually so expansive and descriptive, suddenly stop being so. Phrases like 'on Sunday I vanish into space' appear to Collins (who is in the know), while to Mamie and Georgina he was covering his tracks, with vague and misleading plans. Dickens experts have tracked his movements and found that he was visiting France a great deal, though these visits came to an end in 1865, with the dreadful Staplehurst rail crash, when the train he was travelling in from Folkestone was derailed over the River Beult, with seven carriages plunging into the river. Travel to France never had quite the same appeal again.

HOUSEHOLDS AND SERVANTS

Perhaps Charles Dickens owes his storytelling genius to his grandmother, Elizabeth Dickens. Elizabeth had been a maid to Lady Blandford in Grosvenor Square, but after marrying William Dickens, the butler for Lord Crewe, she had become housekeeper for the Crewe family, and the greatest treat for the Crewe children, Henrietta and Arabella (as Arabella recalled in her adulthood), was to be allowed to make their way to the housekeeper's room, where they listened in rapt attention to 'old Mrs Dickens'. She worked until she was seventy-five, ending her days in a house in Oxford Street, then a residential street. Though she didn't die until Charles was twelve, her skills were not recorded through the Dickens family: indeed, the fact that his grandparents were upper-servants in an aristocratic household was one that, along with Warren's blacking factory, he suppressed until late in his life.

It is, however, an interesting background to this most accomplished of storytellers, whose servant characters are often sympathetic and as strong as the main protagonist. Where, for example, would Mr Pickwick be without Sam Weller? And where might Sam Weller be without Mary Weller, the young servant

Sam Weller in Mr Muzzle's kitchen in *The Pickwick Papers*.

(one of two) in the Chatham household who recorded some of the earliest memories of the young Charles? A nod to her presence in his mind was perhaps made when he called his first, faithful, servant Weller. And Sam Weller's bride, 'the very smart and pretty-faced servant girl', was also called Mary.

When the family moved from Chatham to London, Mary stayed behind and married a shipwright from the dockyard. Accompanying the family to Bayham Street in London was an orphan girl from the Chatham workhouse, the memory of which Dickens drew on for the Marchioness in *The Old Curiosity Shop*.

The matter of servants was of mainly academic – or fictional – interest to Charles, until he maintained his own household. There is a mention of one – an Inns of Court servant – when he was living at 15 Furnival's Inn in 1835 in a letter to John Macrone, who published *Sketches of Boz*, written one November Saturday morning at five o'clock, which also gives an insight into his daily life:

I am writing by candle-light shivering with cold and choaked with smoke. The fire (which has been fed like a furnace at the gas works all night, with a view of my 'early breakfast') has turned unaccountably white and dusty at the very moment when it ought to boil the kettle . . . I think it's rather a disagreeable

Illustration by 'Phiz' (Hablot Browne) of Sam and Tony Weller in *The Pickwick Papers*.

morning but I can't say exactly – because it's so foggy. My laundress who is asthmatic has dived into a closet – I suppose to prevent her cough annoying me – and is emitting from behind the door an uninterrupted succession of the most unearthly and hollow noises I have ever heard.

Certainly when the Dickens family moved to Doughty Street in 1836, there was a need for staff. There were 'tweenies' (as between maids were known) from the orphanage, to act as scullery maids for a weekly wage of 2s. or 2s. 6d., and there must have been the need for a nurse, since two babies were born there. There would have been a cook, a housemaid and later a groom or manservant. Looking at Dickens's account book one can get an idea of the personnel and the wages: the nurse's monthly wage was between £3 and £4 5s.; the cook was paid £3 13s. 6d. per month in 1838; a housemaid was paid 2½ guineas in 1838, rising to 3 guineas in January 1839.

By the time his second son, Walter, was born, Dickens's household had expanded considerably: in the 1841 census return, in which he described himself as 'Gentleman', he declared his household at 1 Devonshire Terrace as consisting of wife and four children, four maidservants and one manservant. In the three years since leaving Furnival's Inn his stock had certainly risen.

The logistics of managing such a household were challenging, particularly with his practice of setting up households in different towns and different countries. An insight into the major task of transplanting a household and the additional responsibilities it entailed can be seen in the case of his family's residence in Genoa in 1844–5. As well as his courier, Louis Roche, the caravan, as he dubbed his entourage, included three female servants – Catherine's maid, Anne Brown; the nurse, Charlotte; and Jane, the cook – all of whom, as he wrote to Forster, dealt with the difficulties of the different language by 'answering with great fluency in English, (very loud: as if the others were only deaf, not Italian)', though a couple of months later he was telling Forster that the servants were beginning 'to pick up scraps of Italian' by the help of a weekly *conversazione* every Sunday at the house of the Governor Marchese Paulucci 'and I think they begin to like their foreigneering life'.

He particularly appreciated the efforts of Jane, who had learned 'the names of all sorts of vegetables, meats, soups, fruits, and kitchen necessaries' by talking to the local laundress. 'She is really a clever woman . . . She is the most contented of all the servants too; and although this house is diabolically supplied, in even such small essentials as the commonest saucepans; she gets on just as she would in Devonshire Terrace, somehow or other; and never makes the least complaint.'

By the following spring she was getting on so well that Dickens passed on surprising 'domestic news' to Maclise: 'You recollect our cook, our nice cook, our good-looking cook; the best Servant as ever trod . . . Yesterday she came up to her mistress, and announced that she was not going to return to England, but intended to be married, and to settle here!!! The Bridegroom is the Governor's Cook: who has been visiting in the kitchen ever since our first arrival.'

They had met at a ball: the governor's servants held one weekly in the summer. Dickens marvelled at the complications of communication – Jane's intended was French, and she could speak no French. He could speak no English, so 'they have courted in Italian'. He was sceptical about their plans to open a nice clean restaurant in Genoa 'which I don't believe . . . for the Genoese have a natural enjoyment of dirt, garlic, and oil'. It was, he thought, 'a great venture on her part, for she is well brought-up: quite delicate in her ideas, full of English notions of cleanliness and decency', such notions clearly being completely at odds with his perception of Italian towns. He feared that she must live 'in some miserable rooms in some miserable neighbourhood'.

Dickens was involved in the bureaucracy of Jane's plans. She had to send to England for her baptism certificate before they could marry – they were of different religions – and for a short while he was optimistic that the bridegroom's religion might stand in the way of their marriage, and so hoped she would return to his household. Over the following months he remained anxious for her, but 'all I can do, is to take care that the Marriage is lawfully and properly solemnized before we depart'.

As it turned out, the marriage, at Lord Holland's villa in Genoa, was only recognized by English law; they had no legal rights in France or Italy. Perhaps because of these difficulties, the couple moved to England in 1851.

Dickens's responsibilities to his servants on this Italian sojourn did not end there. Another had also found true love. 'This is the second of them who has found a lover here; the nurse, Charlotte, having "provided herself" with that commodity the other day. I am in daily expectation of finding that Anne is secretly married to Roche and has a young family.' Later, back in England, he addressed his publishers hoping to find a position for 'a certain young man . . . He is going to marry one of our nurses, who has been with us for six years. He has been servant to Sir George Crawford, whom I know, and who gives him the very best of characters . . .'

He seems to have been a good employer, and made efforts on their behalf, as the above shows. He demanded high standards, writing out instructions for his servants about their duties, but many of them stayed a long time. However, the first servant we know about didn't. One essential from early days was a groom – Dickens did a great deal of riding – and he employed Henry, but in 1838 he had to dismiss him 'for impertinence to his "missis"', though on what count is not recorded. In his stead he took on William Topping, small and red-haired – and thoroughly loyal. He stayed with Dickens for many years, supervising the stable, fetching and delivering (letters often included the request for an immediate reply, and the words 'Topping waits'), and took on other duties, often looking after the London home in the family's long absences. He appears to have managed this competently, judging by the way he dealt with a neighbour over a problem with a smoking chimney.

It was Topping who had charge of the raven Grip, introduced to readers in the preface to *Barnaby Rudge*. He was the first raven kept by Dickens. He lived in the stable (along with an eagle,

Barnaby Rudge with his pet raven, Grip.

which, with the next raven, was dispatched to Edwin Landseer's care when the family went to Italy) but in March 1841, he died. Dickens wrote an elaborate account to Maclise, under an enormous black seal, to forward to Forster because he was 'unable from the state of his feelings to write two letters'.

> *Something remarkable about his eyes occasioned Topping to run for the doctor at twelve. When they returned together my friend was gone. It was the medical gentleman who informed me of his decease . . . I am ever your bereaved friend CD. Kate is as well as can be expected, but terrible low as you may suppose. The children seem rather glad of it. He bit their ankles. But that was play.*

His household was, to some extent, an extension of his family. He talked about his servants with affection and regaled his correspondents with progress reports and anecdotes. When he was travelling round Scotland – a rather rigorous trip – he missed Topping: 'I sigh for Devonshire [Terrace] and Broadstairs . . . and I feel Topping's merits more acutely than I have ever done in my life.' He updated his family, as, for example, when he wrote to his sister Fanny: 'Topping waxes in Years and redness' and then recounted how Timber, the dog he had brought back from America, was stolen from the kitchen. 'He was brought back by Topping & a Policeman – 70 years old, Six feet four inches high & with enormous whiskers whom Topping introduced with these words "Me and this Young Man Sir – We've got him."'

There is a cast of characters throughout the years whom he exhorted, praised and empathized with: Matilda and Mary Anne, two parlourmaids, who mislaid some letters; Isaac Armatage, a page boy; George Belcher, a coachman; James Marsh, the stable man with some minor ailment crying out 'I am dead'; Benjamin Cooper, coachman and groom, a 'steady, stupid sort of highly respectable creature', with seven children, the eldest of whom was working for a mathematical instrument maker and was killed by a coal wagon while on an errand. Dickens describes in affecting detail his death: 'I cannot get it out of my mind.'

But some servants are obviously more important to him than others. One such was Anne Brown, whom Dickens later described as a friend. She was appointed as maid to Catherine – perhaps at Broadstairs, since Dickens once referred to her as 'Anne of Broadstairs' – and accompanied the couple to America. Catherine was at first distressed at the idea of a six-month absence from her children, but Dickens wrote to Forster that, after some anxious discussions, 'Kate is quite reconciled. Anne goes, and is amazingly cheerful and light of heart upon it', and to William Macready that Catherine had been much comforted by 'a stout note' from his brother Fred, who was to live with the children, adding: 'The girl who is going with us, is a moral cork jacket too, and gives great confidence.'

During the privations and exertions of that trip she obviously became close to both of them. She appears to have taken over other duties, for Dickens as well – he remarked once that Anne forgot to pack him some shaving soap – and the tone of affection grew throughout the years. Dickens often sent messages in his letters, asking Catherine to tell her 'that I can't get on at all without her', and referred to her with respect and warmth: on a trip to London when the household was staying in Paris, he wrote to Catherine that he had bought a portmanteau 'which I expect and shall require Anne to fall into fits of admiration'.

The trust he placed in her was clear when Catherine was ill, after the birth of her ninth child, Dora (who later died). Dickens asked her to accompany Catherine to Malvern to take the waters, and wrote to Dr Watson: 'The maid will perfectly understand her errand, and will be sure, (with your kind help) to make the wisest arrangements that the circumstances will admit of.' Anne was used to the family and always knew what to do.

So when, in May 1855, she gave in her notice, he was deeply pained. He lamented to Miss Burdett Coutts: 'I am sorry to say that an invaluable woman who has been with us 16 years – abroad and at home, in America and everywhere – is going to be married.' Her husband-to-be was Edward Cornelius, a French polisher in a pianoforte warehouse. Dickens's farewell letter to her read: 'I cannot tell you how grieved I am to lose you, or what an affectionate remembrance I shall always preserve of your friendship and fidelity during sixteen years.' He presented her with an engraved box, and a cheque for £35. 'I hope you may be very happy, and may think you have reason to recollect me half as kindly as I shall recollect you through the rest of my life.'

But that was not the last he saw of her. She was at Tavistock House at the end of the year, 'when she soon began to cry again, and said she thought she should never "quite settle down"'. And in the following February he wrote to Catherine that Anne intended to come and wait on him on his birthday. He wrote later that she

had, on that occasion, looked 'well and happy, very much brighter altogether'. Within two years, she was back working for him, as housekeeper of Tavistock House, as his letter to Hans Christian Andersen in April 1857 about his future visit makes clear: 'A servant who is our friend also, who lived with us many years and is now married, will be taking care of it; and she will take care of you too, with all her heart.'

He described Anne once as 'an attached woman-servant (more friend to both of us, than a servant) . . . who was, and still is, in Mrs Dickens' confidence', but after his separation from his wife she chose to stay with Dickens. The clear division of interests was shown in October 1857 when, addressing her as 'my old friend', he gave her fateful instructions about 'some little changes' which he would rather not have 'talked about by comparative strangers' to his dressing room – the moving of wash-stands, the dispatch of a chest of drawers and 'the recess of the doorway between the Dressing-Room and Mrs Dickens's room fitted with plain white deal shelves, and closed in with a plain light deal door, painted white'.

Letters about the little tasks he asked of her – such as leaving out mustard poultices for his throat and chest – show that he addressed her as 'My dear Anne'. Her special position in the household is apparent when, some years later, she came to Gad's Hill Place for her daughter Kate to recuperate, though Dickens seems to have had mixed feelings about the daughter: he described her as looking like a Pre-Raphaelite saint in a letter to Wilkie Collins in 1862, but also referred to her as the Demon. He – and his family after his death – made provision for the daughter's education. Though she received the same bequest as other servants, Anne Cornelius was the only servant to be named in his will.

There were other servants he mentioned with affection, such as Charles French, 'a very good and zealous servant'. Dickens entertained his friends with an account of French, in Boulogne, fending off the cats chasing 'our wonderful little Dick' – a canary tamed by Mamie and which lived to be fifteen. The cats 'hide themselves in the most terrific manner, hanging themselves up behind draperies, like bats, and tumbling out in the dead of night with frightful caterwaulings'. French, however, borrowed the landlord's gun and managed to shoot one.

But the following year Dickens was trying to find another position for him, as he had left his service after he suffered a rupture and 'could not carry heavy family trays about'. He wrote to Anthony Panizzi, the librarian at the British Museum, suggesting French for a job in the library. He eventually found a position with Sir Edward Bulwer Lytton at Knebworth, after Dickens commended his qualities, adding that 'he is well used to a literary man's ways'.

In 1862 Dickens was surprised to hear that he had left, as he had thought him 'perfectly satisfied and extremely grateful'. But, he added in an oddly patrician comment for a grandson of servants, 'there is always a latent hankering on the part of this class I believe, to get out of service if possible'. He went on to say he didn't know of a successor. 'An English man-servant who can make his way abroad and makes the best of it, is so very rare an article. And I have been so fortunate in servants, that French and two other men (one dead [Louis Roche] and the other with me now after 18 years [John Thompson]) are all I can be said to have had.'

Louis Roche, a native of Avignon, was a resourceful courier engaged by Dickens for his trips to Italy and Switzerland. Dickens valued him very highly – 'what a prize he is' – and referred to him on occasion as his 'right hand' and 'my good friend and servant'. So well did Roche integrate with the household in Genoa that he oversaw the servants at an important dinner given for the English consul; he had asked, as a special distinction, to be allowed the supreme control of the dessert and he arranged for elaborate ice puddings to be made in the form of fruit.

Before Christmas that year, when Dickens made the long journey back to read *The Chimes* to his friends, Roche accompanied him: 'the brave C continues to be a prodigy. He puts out my clothes at every inn as if I were going to stay there twelve months; calls me at the instant every morning; lights the fire before I get up, gets hold of roast fowls and produces them in coaches at a distance from all other help, at hungry moments; and is invaluable to me.' The only thing Dickens could find to complain of was that he absolutely refused to tip or bribe customs officials – 'in consequence of which that portmanteau of mine has been unnecessarily opened twenty times'.

Roche accompanied the family again to Switzerland the next year and in a letter home Dickens sketched a vignette of a trip up into the mountains. 'If you could have seen him riding a very small mule, up a road exactly like the stairs of Rochester-castle; with a brandy bottle slung over his shoulder, a small pie in his hat, a roast fowl looking out of his pocket, and a mountain staff of six feet long carried cross-wise on the saddle before him . . . He was (next to me) the admiration of Chamonix.'

Coming back to England before Christmas that year, Dickens, demonstrating his loyalty to his employees, remarked: 'I shall bring the Brave, though I have no use of him. He'd die if I didn't.' And later, when living in London again, he remarked on the fact that Roche was constantly back and forth, to play with the children.

Dickens kept Roche's interests at heart, recommending him to others. When he became ill in 1848, with a heart condition, he made sure that he was looked after, seeking Miss Burdett Coutts's help to get him admitted to St George's Hospital. 'I have the deepest interest in the matter, He is a most faithful, affectionate and devoted man.' Roche recovered a little and Dickens wrote to him about his plans that they should go to Spain. But Roche died the following year. As was his wont, Dickens stayed in touch with the family, and in 1850 recommended his brother as a courier.

The longest-serving manservant was John Thompson. He joined the household in the early 1840s and stayed for twenty-four years. In May 1846, when planning his visit to Lausanne

All Moulds, etc., mentioned in the following pages are kept in stock, and can be had wholesale and retail at 30, Mortimer Street, W.

MOULDS FOR ICE PUDDINGS.

All Ice Moulds are made in reputed measure.

PILLAR MOULDS.

No. 1.—FRUIT TOP.	No. 2.—FLUTED TOP.

½	1	1½	2	3 pints.
8s.	9s. 6d.	10s. 6d.	12s. 6d.	16s. each.

½	1	1½	2 pints.
8s. 6d.	9s. 6d.	10s. 6d.	12s. 6d. each.

No. 3.—ROSE TOP.

1	1½	2 pints.
9s. 6d.	10s. 6d.	12s. 6d. each.

No. 4.—STEP TOP.

½	1	1½	2 pints.
7s. 6d.	8s. 9d.	10s. 3d.	11s. 6d.

3 pints, 15s. 3d. each.

No. 17.—OVAL MELON.

7 inches long, 18s. 9d. each.

No. 18.—FRUIT BASKET.

1½ pints, 20s. each.

No. 19.—BASKET OF FRUITS.

Very handsome.   3 pints, 26s. each.

No. 20.—WHEATSHEAF.

8 inches high, 1 quart, 20s. each.

E

Catalogue of elaborate ice pudding moulds, including ones of fruit, of the sort favoured by Dickens's courier, Louis Roche.

John Thompson, Dickens's manservant for many years, lived in rooms above the offices of *All the Year Round*, at 26 Wellington Street – now the Charles Dickens Coffee House.

and letting his house to Sir James Duke, Dickens wrote to agent William Phillips, commending 'my lad John Thompson . . . an excellent footman who perfectly understands his business. If Sir James should want him, I can give him the very strongest recommendation. I would not lose him on my return, if I could help it, on any account.'

John didn't always cover himself with glory, as on an occasion in 1847 when Catherine was in a runaway phaeton at Broadstairs when the pony had bolted down a steep hill. John Thompson threw himself out of the phaeton. 'He says he was thrown, but it could not have been so . . . the man is greatly cut and bruised from head to heel. The women generally have no sympathy for him whatever, and the nurse says, with indignation, how could he go and leave an unprotected female . . .'

He acted at different times as footman, valet and representative. He had duties at both Tavistock House and at the editorial office: Dickens had written to the publisher of *Household Words*, Frederick Evans, in 1850:

> *I wish to mention now, that* in case we ever should *find it expedient to put anybody into the house in Wellington Street, I want to reserve that post for my man John. He has been with me ten years, and is an excellent servant and a most ingenious fellow . . . But he has spoken to me on the subject (with a view, I suppose, to getting married), and I feel that I have no right to stand in his way, but am bound to reward him with what he likes best, if I can.*

When, in 1860, Dickens started his new magazine *All the Year Round* and opened another office in Wellington Street, John moved there, occupying rooms at the top of the building.

Dickens, who had his own accommodation there too, would often send John instructions about meals at the office: 'I shall also be glad to have a little bit of fish and a mutton chop for dinner at the office at half past 4', and reminders about not buying too much. Dickens thought highly of him, telling a friend about his 'cheerful bachelor rooms' at the office, 'with an old servant in charge, who is the cleverest man of his kind in the world, and can do anything – from excellent carpentry to excellent cookery'.

John accompanied Dickens on his reading tours and to Paris. He was fond of doing imitations and when Dickens was reading in Ireland, he told Mamie: 'You should have heard John in my bedroom this morning endeavouring to imitate a bath-man . . . It was more ridiculously unlike the reality than I can express to you, yet he was so delighted with his powers that he went off in the absurdest little gingerbeery giggle, backing into my portmanteau all the time.' When in Paris in January 1863 for a week, Dickens remarked: 'John's amazement at, and appreciation of, Paris are indescribable. He goes about with his mouth open, staring at everything and being tumbled over by everybody.' Dickens left him

there while he went off for a week, presumably to see Ellen, and approvingly reported to Wilkie Collins that John 'has *no* British prejudices', which was remarkable in a man unacquainted with the language, and who had 'to subsist wholly on Pantomime'.

After the Staplehurst railway accident, when his travelling companion injured her arm – a delicate situation – John was entrusted with errands of mercy and given responsibility for choosing treats: 'Take Miss Ellen tomorrow morning, a little basket of fresh fruit, a jar of clotted cream from Tuckers, and a chicken, a pair of pigeons, or some nice little bird. Also on Wednesday morning, and on Friday morning, take her some other things of the same sort – making a little variety each day.'

He was in a privileged position, and Dickens, always appreciative, was very protective of him, concerned when he seemed low; when he fell off a platform on a tour; over the

This modest wine cellar at Doughty Street was succeeded by much grander ones at Gad's Hill Place, though Dickens was bothered by servants pilfering champagne, until he instituted an elaborate system of keys.

officiousness on the part of magazine staff towards him; and especially when he was very ill in May 1864. Dickens went back in the evening from the London home he was renting to check on him and found 'that diabolical wife [John's] *and her sister* being left to watch him, got blind drunk on gin instead'. He charged Wills to make this known 'in its fullest atrocity to everybody at the office, and let everyone be strictly charged never on any pretence to let the woman into the house'.

So it must have been all the more devastating when in 1866 he discovered that John was a thief. Eight sovereigns were stolen at Wellington Street, and then replaced. Dickens called in Scotland Yard. 'It was the clumsy manner of the restoration, that most helped the discovery of the culprit.' It turned out that he had been stealing for some time. 'It has so shocked me, that I have had to walk more than usual before I could walk myself into composure again,' he told Lavinia Watson. It was 'a horrible business'.

For Dickens, this must have felt like a sad betrayal, and a rejection, for as he wrote to his sister Letitia in 1861 when he was providing help, support and advice after the death of her husband, Dickens's constant adviser, Henry Austin, 'a good servant – especially to you, to whom a good and tried servant would stand in the light of a friend – is not a thing to throw away'.

But with generosity of spirit, he wrote to his sister-in-law Georgina to ask her to keep the news from the other servants ('Say that you believe John is going into some small business – anything of that kind') and to Mamie that no third person 'who knew him through his old long service should witness John's shame'. He arranged, with his usual efficiency, to replace him at *All the Year Round* with Ellen Hedderley, once in service at Gad's Hill and now a widow, as housekeeper. Two days later, he was asking Georgina to tell Ellen about her quarters at *All the Year Round* – a good sitting room at the bottom of the house, three bright airy rooms adjoining each other at the top, coals, candles and a guinea a week – and telling Wills about the new arrangements: 'She has "very nice furniture", she says, for her own rooms. I told her that she would find the kitchen furnished for her.'

He replaced John with Henry Scott who, the following year, Dickens was commending as a 'skilful valet' and 'as a dresser he is perfect. Punctual, quiet, and quick.' He was 'always cheerful, and useful, and ready', though in August that year, Dickens remarked that Scott, summoned to Wellington Street, was 'horribly disappointed by being brought up from Gad's; where he had settled himself among the women-servants, the fowls, boys, horses, cricket paraphernalia, and dogs with intense enjoyment'.

Dickens was not averse to playing the part of a servant himself at times. James Fields, his American publisher, described an outing with Dickens which ended up with a picnic at Cooling graveyard, where Dickens spread a tablecloth over ' a good flat gravestone' in one corner: 'Having spread the table after the most approved style, he suddenly disappeared behind the wall for a moment, [and] transformed himself by the aid of a towel and a napkin into a first-class head waiter.'

Though there were irritations over servants – bottles of champagne disappeared from the cellars at Gad's Hill Place until he designed with Georgina an elaborate system of secreting the cellar keys – Dickens remained attentive and interested in his households until the end. At Gad's Hill, he instructed his servants in making buttonholes for each guest, of scarlet geranium with a bit of the leaf and a frond of maidenhair fern, and taught a special way of folding serviettes, as one of his maids from the last years remembered: 'Lord Darnley's servants were always anxious to learn how the folding was done; they never discovered the secret'. And his servants appreciated him. According to Mamie, they were often 'convulsed with laughter at his droll remarks'. He told Annie Fields, wife of his American publisher, in a letter how on his return from America the village had put out flags, and his servants, not to be outdone, 'had dressed the house so that every brick was hidden. They had asked Mamie's permission to "ring the alarm-bell" (!) when master drove up, but Mamie, having some slight idea that the compliment might awaken master's sense of the ludicrous, had recommended bell abstinence.'

William Hughes in his *A Week's Tramp in Dickensland* gives an account by a parlourmaid who had worked at Gad's Hill for four years. 'On one occasion the dinner lift broke, smashing the crockery and bruising her arm. Mr Dickens jumped up quickly and said "Never mind the breakage; is your arm hurt?" As it was painful, he immediately applied arnica to the bruise, and gave her a glass of port wine.'

There was a later problem at the *All the Year Round* office when a senior employee of the magazine, William Johnson, was found to be pilfering, to the shock of Dickens and the great distress of Wills. Dickens set himself to raise Wills's spirits about it, in the process giving an insight into his attitude.

If we try to do our duty by people we employ; by exacting their proper service from them on the one hand, and treating them with all possible consistency, gentleness, and consideration on the other, we know that we do right. Their doing wrong cannot change our doing right, and that should be enough for us.
So I have given my *feathers a shake, and am all right again. Give* your *feathers a shake, and take a cheery flutter into the air of Hertfordshire.*

The graves at Cooling, which inspired the early scenes of *Great Expectations* – and a favourite spot for picnics, at which Dickens would act as a waiter.

HOME AGAIN TO KENT:
1860–70

Though he was born in Portsmouth, and lived most of his life in London, Dickens's true home seemed to be Kent, where he had spent five years of his childhood. He frequently made trips back to Chatham and Rochester in his adult years. 'There was nothing', he said in one essay, 'more picturesque to the eye, and agreeable to the fancy, than an old Cathedral town', and so he returned to write articles and stories. His first thought on finishing *David Copperfield* was to visit the area he considered home. He took friends to explore the town and the countryside: the walk between Maidstone and Rochester was, he asserted, one of the finest in the land. And he was walking here, through Higham, on his birthday in 1855, when he saw Gad's Hill Place was for sale.

Gad's Hill Place held a particular place in his affections for its childhood memories: 'when I was a small boy down in these parts, I thought it the most beautiful house (I suppose because of its famous old Cedar Trees) ever seen'. He wrote in *The Uncommercial Traveller* about seeing the house for the first time, as 'a queer small boy'. The 'mansion of dull red brick, with a little

Gad's Hill Place, the house in Higham that Dickens had known since childhood.

weathercock-surmounted cupola, on the roof, and a bell hanging in it' of Scrooge's childhood home is remarkably like Gad's Hill Place. Forster said in his *Life*:

> *Very often had we travelled past it together, many years before it became his home, and never without some allusion to what he told me when first I saw it in his company, that amid the recollections connected with his childhood it held always a prominent place, for upon first seeing it . . . with his father . . . he had been promised that he might himself live in it or some such house when he came to be a man, if he would only work hard enough. Which for a long time was his ambition.*

Now, while he was on his birthday ramble, he saw this 'little Freehold to be sold. The spot and the very house are literally "a dream of my childhood", and I should like to look at it . . .'

Gad's Hill Place is now – and has been since 1924 – a school, but it is still easy to see what attracted Dickens and his father to it, with its pleasant proportions, bell turret and porch with wooden seats. It was built in 1779 by Alderman Thomas Stevens, a brewer

View from the Roof of Dickens's House at Gad's Hill

Sketch by Frederic Kitton of the view from the roof of Gad's Hill Place.

of Rochester (Dickens was later to discover that it had 'an amazing cellar'). 'The whole stupendous property', as Dickens later referred to it, is in a fine situation, with Cobham woods and park behind the house, and prospects of the Thames and the Medway, with Rochester and its old castle and cathedral. But at that point, in the middle of the nineteenth century, it was a slightly neglected run-down house with two tenants, the Reverend Joseph Hindle and his daughter.

Dickens obtained the particulars of the house from the agent, perhaps as a sort of daydream, though he asked Wills to come down and look at it with him a couple of days later. In fact, that expedition was deferred, for the day it was planned was the day he received a letter from the former Maria Beadnell, his first love, and his mind was immediately elsewhere. Wills went later and his report was such that, despite his strong attachment to the house,

Dickens appeared to dismiss the idea of purchasing it: 'It is clear to me that its merits resolve themselves into the view and the spot . . . I consider the matter quite disposed of – finally settled in the negative – and to be thought no more about.'

But then, by chance, Wills met at supper Miss Eliza Lynn, a contributor to Dickens's journals, and now co-owner of Gad's Hill Place after the death of her father early that year. She was keen to sell, and Dickens's interest was rekindled. As had so often happened in the past, he asked his brother-in-law Henry Austin to ascertain the condition and value of the house. As usual, he saw improvements that could be made, wondering if, by reslating the roof, it would be possible to increase the size of the low garrets.

By August, Dickens, who was spending the summer in Boulogne, had authorized Wills to offer £1,500. He was determined not to offer more than £1,700 because of the necessary alterations. He saw it as an investment, a property to rent out in a newly accessible part of the country, and enthused to Forster about the advantage of the new railway line that connected Higham with the seaside. For an outlay of another £300, he told Forster, he would be able to let it out for £100 a year.

Negotiations dragged on for several months. Early in 1856, he complained to Wills that the purchase seemed to be 'a sort of amateur Chancery Suit which will never be settled'. But in March, Gad's Hill Place was his for £1,790.

Though he seems to have had mixed feelings about it during the process of purchase, once it was his he took his son Charley to see it, along with Wilkie Collins and Mark Lemon. Charley recalled: 'My father full of pride at his new position as a Kentish freeholder and making all manner of jokes at his own expense . . . We lunched at the Falstaff Inn opposite, and walked to Gravesend to dinner, full of delighted anticipation of the country life to come.'

The deeds for Gad's Hill Place. They were conveyed some months after Dickens had paid for it.

Dickens was full of proprietorial pride about the countryside, which 'against every disadvantage of the season, is beautiful', and the house 'so old fashioned, cheerful, and comfortable that it is really pleasant to look at'. He agreed that the 'good old Rector' who had lived there for twenty-six years could remain until Lady Day the following year, after which the house would be refurbished. He wrote eagerly to Miss Burdett Coutts about his intention to make it 'clean and pretty in the papering and painting way, and then to furnish it in the most comfortable manner, and let it by the month whenever I can'. When he could not, it would be a useful weekend retreat, he said, for himself and Charley.

So early in 1857, he commissioned Austin to find a builder to start work immediately the day after the tenants moved out, on 26 March. The roof was to be repaired and to be raised six feet to allow more room in the top rooms. With his usual drive and determination, he wanted the work done fast: '(any taste for Circumlocution being inadmissible)'. He wanted it ready for Catherine's birthday in May.

At different times, sometimes with Catherine, he stayed at the Wates Hotel in Gravesend or at the Sir John Falstaff Inn across the road, so 'that I may have an eye on the little repairs at Gad's Hill'. He was, as always, intimately involved with the work. He told Miss Burdett Coutts that 'I have devised an immense number of small inventions . . . There *is* a little study (I am sorry to say that the merit of hewing it out of a china-closet is Mr Austin's) – but you must see it.' The house would be full, he promised, of 'the ingenious devices of the inimitable writer'. (Tommy Traddles, David Copperfield's friend, had the same skill in making 'ingenious arrangements' to accommodate his possessions in his tiny room.) Mamie wrote later: 'He invented all sorts of neat and

Kitton's sketch of the Sir John Falstaff Inn, across the road from Gad's Hill Place.

clever contrivances, and was never happier than when going about the house with a hammer and nails doing some wonderful piece of carpentering.'

He began the furnishing with a certain amount of cunning, by sending his servant John to buy pieces as if for himself, and thus acquiring things at 'a very fair advantage . . . and permitting him to bring them away ignobly in Vans, Cabs, barrow, trucks and costermonger's trays. If you should meet such a thing as a Mahogany dining table or two marble washing-stands, in a donkey cart anywhere, or in a cats'-meat cart . . . you may be sure the property is mine.' He was enjoying himself.

He was soon calling himself the Inimitable Kentish Freeholder. He was proud of the historical connections – a plaque on the landing carried a quotation from *Henry IV, Part I*: 'But, my lads, my lads, to-morrow morning, by four o'clock, early at Gadshill: there are pilgrims going to Canterbury with rich offerings, and traders riding to London with fat purses: I have visors for you all, you have horses for yourselves.'

He was soon telling everyone that this was the identical spot where Falstaff ran away and the countryside was 'in all its general features' what it was in Shakespeare's time: 'The robbery was committed before the door, on the ground now covered by the room in which I write,' he wrote to de Cerjat. 'A little rustic alehouse, called the Sir John Falstaff, is over the way, has been over the way ever since, in honour of the event.'

He was also boasting of his alterations: 'My little place is a grave red brick house (time of George the First, I suppose), which I have added to and stuck bits upon in all manner of ways, so that it is pleasantly irregular, and as violently opposed to all architectural ideas, as the most hopeful man could possibly desire.' 'You will hardly know Gad's Hill again,' he wrote to Forster soon after the renovations. 'I am improving it so much – yet I have no interest in the place.' But Forster added that 'continued ownership brought increased liking; he took more and more interest in his own improvements, which were just the kind of occasional occupation and resource his life most wanted in its next seven or eight years'.

The family visited to celebrate Catherine's birthday there and then moved lock, stock and birds into the house on 1 June – not without incident, as they appear to have arrived via Sussex, having caught the wrong train (they were charge of a 'stupefied John'). It was the beginning of a country life, with horses, and dogs of all sizes, from the Pomeranian Mrs Bouncer, Mamie's dog, to Newfoundlands and a St Bernard.

Less than a week later there was a domestic disaster, as the well ran dry, presumably unused to the demand from such a large household. As usual Dickens appealed to Henry Austin, but there was no easy solution. After digging for water for some weeks, they had to try boring. Towards the end of July, he was writing to Austin again in moderate tones: 'I really begin to think we are a little unfortunate here.' Then there was an additional problem of blocked drains, which required two cesspools. Things became a little more frantic: 'The cook in tears – garden chaotically dragged up by the roots – everybody tearing their own hair and mine too . . .'

In August he wrote triumphantly to Austin: 'At last, I am happy to inform you we have got at a famous spring!!' It was clear and apparently exhaustless, but the arrival of a pump was delayed, causing 'the aggravation of knowing that the water was at the bottom of the well – but still paying for that accursed water-cart that comes jogging backwards and forwards – and of looking at the dry bath, morning after morning'. It eventually took six men to fit the pump, which he likened to a railway terminus – 'so iron and so big'. He calculated then that the first glassful of water drunk at the surface would cost £200. The cost in the end was 'absolutely frightful' – £300 – though he took comfort from it increasing the value of the property.

In the summer of the next year, new problems arose when the pump broke yet again: 'And the Rochester man says "He'd rather have nothink to do with that 'ere infernal ma-sheen",' Dickens wrote to Austin. 'Pray help me! Pray, pray save me from bankruptcy and Despair!' Apart from anything else, the pump required much manpower, and the men hired had run away, one after another. Dickens decided that the machine must be altered: 'I must establish a revolving poney.' As Hughes recounted in *A Week's Tramp in Dickensland*, he actually saw the horse-drawn pump in operation, courtesy of the then owner of Gad's Hill Place. The impressively huge machinery can be seen today behind Eastgate House in Rochester, moved there in 1973.

Naturally, none of these problems hindered Dickens's hospitality, though he regretted one of his first visitors: Hans Christian Andersen, described by Katie as a 'bony bore', expected for two weeks, stayed for five. Afterwards Dickens put up a card saying, 'Hans Andersen slept in this room for five weeks – which seemed to the family AGES.'

By the following year, after Dickens's separation from Catherine in 1858, the mood of the house had changed substantially. He installed his family at Gad's Hill, with its 'triumvirate of housekeepers' – Mamie, Katie and Georgie – 'all three devotedly attached'. But all was not well: Katie continued to see her mother, and Dickens could barely speak to her after these visits. In 1860 Katie left home, to marry Charles Collins, Wilkie's younger brother. The wedding day was filled with frenetic activity at Gad's Hill after the couple's early departure – games on the lawn, a trip to Rochester Castle and much apparent jollity – but later Mamie

Dickens with his daughters Mamie and Katie in the garden of Gad's Hill Place.

In 1860 too he decided to sell Tavistock House. Once the decision was made he sold it rapidly, to a solicitor, James Davis: 2,000 guineas for a thirty-six-year term. The bargain was made in five minutes, he said triumphantly, and the conveyances were executed and money paid within as many days. He set about making arrangements to transfer books and the choicer furniture to Gad's Hill. He issued information to the new owner about the communal gardener and advice about the careful locking of the gate. He commissioned Benjamin Lillie to take down pictures and transfer bookcases, with comments on embellishments to be added with a view to the look of it – he wanted them to be 'substantial to the eye' – and on the papering and painting: the remaining woodwork visible was to be painted to imitate dark wood, and the ceiling paper was to match.

At the same time, he needed to help the widow of his brother Alfred, who had died suddenly. He organized it so that she would look after his widowed mother, paying for their house at 4 Grafton Terrace until his mother's death in 1863. He was also issuing directions to his manservant John about rearranging and decorating the rooms at the office: a stove – that didn't smoke – was to be installed, and he asked John to provide samples of wallpaper for him to look at, so that he could decide on a cheerful décor.

Impatient, as always, for things to be sorted and in order swiftly, he nevertheless had to defer a visitor in September, as he was still 'beset with Workmen. They are only making bookshelves, but might be making Houses of Parliament.' Later still, he was telling Mamie that everything was a great success, but he was driven out of his study by the smell of paint and had to write in the spare room.

His new plan was to live at Gad's Hill Place for seven months in the year, thus always being there during the boys' holidays, and to take a small furnished house in town during the other five, only 'for Mamie's sake'. He himself could always, and did often, retreat to his bachelor rooms at the office.

found Dickens weeping over Katie's wedding dress: 'But for me, Katie would not have left home.'

Perhaps because he was back in the surroundings so familiar from his youth, this is the year when Dickens began to write *Great Expectations*, which opens in a graveyard based on that of Cooling, just down the road. Written in the first person and with autobiographical elements, like *David Copperfield*, it was produced in weekly instalments for *All the Year Round* instead of monthly ones, as there were problems with sales of the magazine. It was a huge success – and when the book was published the following year, it had gone into a fourth edition by the following August.

The first 'very pretty' London house in 1861 was at 3 Hanover Terrace, Regent's Park. In the 1861 census, conducted while they were in this house, Georgina was somewhat unflatteringly called 'Servant housekeeper'; Dickens – 'Gentleman' in the 1841 census – was now described as 'Author, Novelist, Essayist & Editor'. Interestingly, and uncharacteristically, when the tenancy ended, he was sent an 'astonishing' bill by the agent for damages to the house: the granddaughter of Sir Charles Rowley, its owner, noted that 'the house was left in a shocking condition owing to the various uncontrolled dogs Dickens had with him'.

The following year he avoided agents, as he did a swap with the niece of a friend, Mrs George Hogge, for 16 Hyde Park Gate, but though it was conveniently close to Kensington Gardens and riding (for Mamie), he disliked it intensely, calling it 'the nastiest little house'. He even blamed the house on his inability to settle down to his new novel – already named *Our Mutual Friend*, but not actually begun until 1863: 'this odious little house seems to have stifled and darkened my intention'.

In 1864, he investigated several houses thoroughly and conscientiously before settling on 57 Gloucester Place, in Hyde Park, the area he favoured for his last three London homes for its healthy properties: 16 Somer's Place in 1865; 6 Southwick Place in 1866; and 5 Hyde Park Place in 1870. He could always escape to Wellington Street, or elsewhere in one of his discreet absences to see Ellen. But Gad's Hill Place remained his bedrock, and he never lost his interest in making improvements to it and acquisitions for it, from a sundial set upon one of the balustrades of the destroyed old Rochester Bridge and presented to him by the contractor for the works, to the meadow behind the house – used for cricket matches and races, as on Boxing Day 1866 – 'because that ground, being freehold, would manifestly increase the value of my little place'.

In 1861, he was concerned with an equally important asset, writing to Edmund Yates – a friend, but this was in his official capacity in the Secretary's Department of the Post Office – to

Dickens standing in the porch of his new home.

make a pitch for something close to his heart: 'I think that no one, seeing the place, can well doubt that my house at Gad's Hill, is the place for the letter box. The wall is accessible by all sorts and conditions of men, on the bold high road; and the house altogether is the great landmark of the neighbourhood.' He obviously won the argument, as the following year he broke off a letter to Wilkie Collins by saying that he must 'get this into the box before it is cleared at the gate here'.

His continuing pleasure in the simply domestic can still be seen in *Our Mutual Friend* in the light-hearted discussion between Eugene Wrayburn and Mortimer Lightwood on domestic virtues, and Eugene's description of 'the little narrow room – which was completely and neatly fitted as a kitchen. "See!" said Eugene, "miniature flour-barrel, rolling-pin, spice-box, shelf of brown jugs, chopping-board, coffee-mill, dresser elegantly furnished with crockery, saucepans, roasting-jack, a charming kettle, an armoury of dish-covers. The moral influence of these objects in forming the domestic virtues, may have an immense influence upon me."'

The summer that he was writing this Dickens decided to extend the drawing room, which, he told Lillie, 'would involve some re-decoration of those rooms, and your former work was so very pretty'. In due course, he reported on progress to Wilkie Collins: 'The Girders were both got up by 8 o'Clock at night. It was ticklish work – nine men gasping, snuffling, heaving, snorting, balancing themselves on bricks, and tumbling over each other. But it really was well done and with great cheerfulness and spirit, to which three gallons of beer, judiciously thrown in, imparted a festive air.'

Though he wasn't happy about the mirror Lillie installed, as it distorted the room, and demanded his immediate attention to it as the decoration and furnishing of the room had to be completed in a fortnight, he later paid the bill of £184 10s. 6d. with a complimentary letter, expressing his satisfaction with Lillie's work – and his satisfaction in being able to tell him so. And, naturally, he told his friends all about it. In his next letter to de Cerjat, he wrote: 'I've altered this place very much since you were here and have made a very pretty (I think unusually pretty) Drawing Room.'

Other work included asking Lillie to replace most of the windows with the 'best plate glass', and Joseph Couchman, master builder of Strood, to repair chimneys and make new bedrooms in the roof; he made alterations inside as well, deciding that his study at the back of the house should become a billiard room, and asking Franklin Homan, cabinet-maker and upholsterer of Rochester, to widen the door. Homan remembered one other commission in that room: referring to a one-sided couch in the billiard room, Dickens said to Homan, 'Whenever I see that couch, it make me think the window is squinting,' and he instructed him to make a window seat.

He moved his workplace to the front room, which had large windows overlooking the drive. Now the headmaster's study at Gad's Hill School, it still has a sense of Dickens, and retains the dummy books ranging up over the door and nearby walls. These include *Hansard's Guide to Refreshing Sleep*, *Growler's Gruffology*, *Paxton's Bloomers*, *History of Middling Ages*, *The Gunpowder Magazine* and *Life and Letters of the Learned Pig*.

The paint was barely dry on each improvement before he was cajoling friends to visit to admire them. He wrote to Edward Bulwer Lytton: 'I have turned the house upside down and inside out since you were here, and have carved new rooms out of places then non-existent.' Telling de Cerjat about the billiard room, he urged him to 'Come and play a match with me.'

One of the greatest and best additions was as a result of a gift: a two-storey Swiss chalet presented to him by the actor Charles Fechter at Christmas in 1864. It arrived in 58 boxes containing 94 pieces. Dickens suggested that his guests help put it together, but then had to summon Fechter's French carpenter, M. Godin, from the Lyceum Theatre to help. Couchman, the local builder, had to finish putting it up, after getting help from Henry Dickens in translating the French names on the pieces.

It was erected in the shrubbery 'Wilderness' across the road: access was easy as he had, some years earlier, commissioned his brother Alfred to design a spacious tunnel under the road, lined with brick – the construction of which Dickens likened to a spectator sport: 'I was at one time honoured with the attendance of as many as seven and twenty, who were looking at six [workmen].' The tunnel is still accessible, though it now leads to a locked gate. The chalet, with its six windows on the top floor covered by louvred shutters, and balcony with delicate rails and a lion couchant, can still be seen in the grounds of Eastgate House in Rochester, just as it appeared then, though it needs restoration and a fund has been set up to find £100,000.

This was where in the last few years of his life Dickens worked, at his sloping desk on the table, among the trees. He wrote to Annie Fields, the wife of his American publisher, about it:

I have put five mirrors in the chalet where I write, and they reflect and refract, in all kinds of ways, the leaves that are quivering at the windows, and the great fields of waving corn, and the sail-dotted river. My room is up among the branches of the trees; and the birds and the butterflies fly in and out, and the green branches shoot in at the open windows, and the lights and shadows of the clouds come and go with the rest of the company. The scent of the flowers, and indeed of everything that is growing for miles and miles, is most delicious.

LEFT The Swiss chalet, presented to Dickens by an actor friend, Charles Fechter, and erected in the shrubbery known as the Wilderness. It now stands in the grounds of Eastgate House in Rochester.

RIGHT The steps from the garden down to the tunnel beneath the road leading to the Wilderness and the chalet.

For his small granddaughter, though, there was something rather eerie about the chalet. Mary Angela, Charley's eldest child, recalled that when he took himself to the chalet to write 'the haze of the mysterious rose about him in my little mind . . . I can feel myself, now, creeping indoors, when I had been sent to play in the garden, because the thought of that little house among the trees, with its solitary occupant, haunted me . . .'

It seems a perceptive attitude for a child, for a striking thing about Dickens in this decade is that, though he was so convivial, so hospitable and so successful, he was solitary. There were many anxieties and sadnesses: disillusionment with his family – he wrote to Wilkie Collins in October 1866 that he expected to be presented with a pewter watch 'for having brought up the largest family ever known, with the smallest disposition to do anything for themselves'; the many deaths of close friends; concerns over Georgina's health; and concerns over his own as, in 1866, he was diagnosed with 'great irritability of the heart' – something that he seems to have been, metaphorically, suffering from for some years. For percolating throughout his existence were worries over Ellen; his letters to Wilkie Collins in the early 1860s are full of allusions to 'miserable anxieties'.

The shocking railway accident at Staplehurst in 1865, in which he came so close to death (also nearly losing an episode of *Our Mutual Friend*) and which left him horribly shaken for some time (indeed, perhaps permanently), disclosed what he had been keeping secret for so long, as he was travelling with Ellen and her mother. She had been living in Boulogne, after which she moved to the more mundane location of Slough (and he, 'Charles Tringham', also rented a cottage in the High Street), and then in 1867 to a genteel house, rented by Dickens, at 16 Linden Grove, opposite Nunhead Cemetery in Peckham. Though he remained publicly discreet, gradually he took more people into his confidence about her. His assistant Wills sometimes acted as go-between. But she stayed in the background, and he remained alone. For a man who, as Mamie said

Ellen Ternan, the young actress whom Dickens met in 1856 and who became a close companion.

after his death, was a 'home-man' in every respect – 'no man was so inclined naturally to derive his happiness from home affairs' – this must have made a difficult life.

But it was always a full one. Apart from the books, there were the reading tours – naturally he designed his portable reading table – which were becoming very lucrative, but hugely demanding: the one planned for 1866 for fifty readings earned him more than £3,000, though perhaps what motivated him as much as the money was the tremendous reception he received almost everywhere. He commented: 'the affectionate regard of

Dickens at one of his public readings.

submitting articles, stories and poetry of their own or of their daughters; reading friends' books, generously and enthusiastically dispensing praise and comment, for example on Bulwer Lytton's *Lost Tales of Miletus*; as well as finding time to give a recipe for salad dressing, and one for dog food (oatmeal, barley meal and mangelwurzel, with the possible addition of a sheep's head).

Work was always pre-eminent in his life, but he continued to urge his friends to visit. Guests would be met at the station by the basket phaeton or the brougham (a present from Wills), drawn by a horse called Newman Noggs (after the clerk in *Nicholas Nickleby*) and adorned with Norwegian musical bells (a present from another friend). Their journey to the house would take them through hop and corn fields. There would be good food: a typical menu included pheasants with oysters, sweetbreads with peas, saddle of mutton and truffles, ginger pudding, mince pies and orange water ice. There would be charades, music, memory games, dancing, cards. On New Year's Eve, Dickens would open the front door so that everyone could hear the bells of the church and then, according to Mamie, would lead the dancing, usually partnering the cook. Despite the shadows in his life, he was always entertaining and careful of the happiness of his guests.

Henry Chorley, a critic and novelist, wrote in his reminiscences that at Gad's Hill 'in every room I found a table covered with writing materials, headed notepaper, envelopes, cut quill-pens, wax, matches, sealing-wax and all scrupulously neat and orderly'. George Dolby, manager of Dickens's last reading tours, expanded on this:

A peculiarity of the household was the fact that, except at table, no servant was ever seen about. This was because the requirements of life were always ready to hand, especially in the bedrooms. Each of these rooms contained the most comfortable of beds, a sofa and an easy-chair, cane-bottomed chairs – in which Dickens had a great belief, always preferring to use one

the people exceeds all bounds and is shown in every way. The audiences do everything but embrace me, and take as much pains with the Readings as I do.'

He was wholeheartedly engaged with *All the Year Round*, commenting, editing, rewriting, and amending each article. He had to take on the thankless task, as literary executor for a clergyman friend, of publishing a book of the strangest fragments of religious opinions. He was looking after members of his family; raising funds for widows of friends; taking up cases of people fallen into difficult circumstances; dispensing advice – very bluntly – to people

The Old Leather Bottle at Cobham, another favourite place for excursions, and which featured in *The Pickwick Papers*.

himself – a large-sized writing table, profusely supplied with envelopes of every conceivable size and description, and an almost daily change of new quill pens. There was a miniature library of books in each room, comfortable fire in winter, with a shining copper kettle in each fireplace, and on the side-table, cups, saucers, tea-caddy, teapot.

The pleasures of the day were, as Dolby said, always arranged methodically: 'Mr Dickens was always systematic.' There might be a trip to the Old Leather Bottle at Cobham, bowls or croquet on the lawns in the afternoon, billiards at night. Dickens went to bed at midnight, having first deputized someone to go round the house and 'see the gas goes out all right, as well as taking care of the keys of the sideboard until morning'.

When the Fieldses visited here, after London (where Dickens had taken them on a two-hour tour of the Post Office, 'to see the hurry and rush of letters!'), he hired a Pickwick-style coach, with postilions in red jackets, for an excursion, just as he had with Longfellow in 1868. He also took them on picnics. Dolby recalled the care that attended such picnics, with 'a quantity of small baskets in which were parcelled all the necessaries for midday meal – nothing forgotten, not even the pepper, salt, mustard and corkscrew'. Another guest recollected rambles

led discursively among scenes with which, thanks to him, you had long ago become familiar – over Rochester Bridge where Mr Pickwick moralized within view of the time-worn ruins of the Castle; past the Bull Inn on the staircase of which Mr Jingle infuriated Dr Slammer; through Cobham Park to which by a pass-key, the master of Gad's Hill Place had the privilege of perpetual access; under the wall of the churchyard where Pip first met Magwitch . . .

There were more sedentary pursuits too. In summer, guests were encouraged to sit in the gardens full of honeysuckle, nasturtiums, mignonette and geraniums. Mamie spoke of Dickens's 'passion for colour, so the garden was planted with the brightest coloured flowers, the two beds in the front being filled with scarlet geraniums – his favourite flower – which made a splendid blaze'. If it were winter, according to Percy Fitzgerald, Gad's Hill Place was a 'real-life Dingley Dell', with its 'cheerful red curtain, illuminated from within, and giving a promise of the snug blazing fires, and logs, and maybe a comforting glass'.

Mary Boyle, a long-time friend since he met her at Rockingham Castle, particularly remembered 'the drawing-room games in which he took so much delight, the brightest conversation'. There was 'an absurd charade' in which he played a sailor 'dancing a preposterous hornpipe with as much humorous detail as if he had had days of rehearsal to work it up instead of comparatively few minutes'. He also 'really did' play the games of How, When and Where and Yes and No as played in *A Christmas Carol*, and 'a special memory game which was really hard work by reason of the extra attention and care which is required – as if his life depended on his success'. Annie Fields, one of his last guests, said: 'it was wonderful the flow of spirits Charles Dickens has *for a sad man*'.

Though family and friends tried to dissuade him – they were concerned about his health – he determined to undertake a six-month reading tour of America. 'The prize looks so large!' he said: he was offered £10,000 but in the event he earned around double that. From there, he commissioned the Rochester cabinet-maker Franklin Homan to do some work on the bedrooms at Gad's Hill. He asked for the curtains separating the dressing rooms to be of Indian patterned chintz. But when, on his return, he saw them completed, he said: 'It strikes me as if the room was about to have its hair cut – but it's my fault, it must be altered.' So they became crimson damask curtains. Dickens was 'one of the nicest customers I ever met in my life, so thoroughly precise and methodical,' Homan said. 'He knew exactly what he wanted and gave his instructions accordingly. He expected everyone who served him to be equally exact and punctual.'

Despite his ill health – the 'irritability of the heart' and a deeply painful inflammation of his left foot, which often disabled him from walking – he began his farewell tour of Britain, which had 100 engagements (agreed fee £8,000), in the

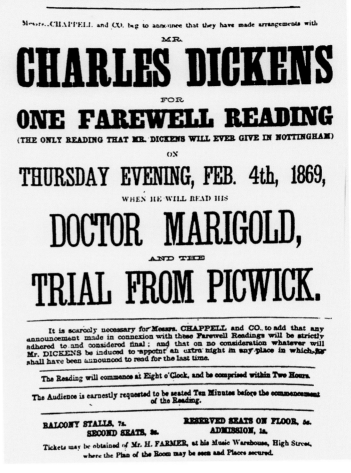

A poster from Dickens's farewell reading tour.

autumn of 1869. His ailments mounted, added to which, in a hangover from the Staplehurst accident, he frequently suffered fits of terror during the rail journeys. But he was still alert to the possibilities of improvements wherever he went. Remarking that George Dolby's house in Ross-on-Wye, though pleasantly furnished, 'like the best sort of Railway hotel', was the coldest house he'd ever been in, he pronounced that it was very much

The much-longed-for conservatory, installed at Gad's Hill Place shortly before Dickens died.

was editing *All the Year Round*, a more onerous task as the invaluable Wills had had to retire after an accident the previous year. And he was writing his last book, *The Mystery of Edwin Drood*. The success of the first instalment, in March, exceeded all his previous works with 40,000 printed – 10,000 more than *Our Mutual Friend*.

He did not return to Gad's Hill until the end of May, but he had been making plans from afar for the garden and the house. He had employed a new head gardener (there were four gardeners altogether) and he gave Charles Fechter a list of the changes: a forcing house for flowers; melon frames, cucumber frames and mushroom beds to produce every week of the year; a hundred loads of gravel put upon the paths to raise them; a model stable with zinc fittings, and water laid on for every horse. Then inside the house, 'a new staircase rears its modest form (gilded and brightly painted) . . . all the upper landing is inlaid in a banquet of precious-woods and the nice parlour maid is going to be married in a fortnight at Higham Church'.

His final magnificent improvement was the addition of – at last – a conservatory. It was 'Brilliant. But expensive. With foundations of horrible solidity.' He had long coveted one and now he had a grand structure with arched windows, leading from his dining room and connecting with the drawing room. He showed it off to Katie, on her visit on 7 June, saying: 'Well, Katie, now you see POSITIVELY the last improvement at Gad's Hill.' The next day he fixed up Chinese lanterns in his conservatory and sat in there, smoking a cigar and enjoying his long-desired acquisition.

On the last full day of his life, he worked in his chalet on *The Mystery of Edwin Drood*, adding a description of Cloisterham, as he dubbed Rochester in this book:

'wanting in cheap contrivances that would make it seem larger and be more commodious. I could do wonders with it, and not spend more than £20.'

His spirit, indomitable as ever, carried him through, to great and affectionate acclaim everywhere, until an onset of paralysis caused his doctor to insist he cancel remaining engagements and forswear rail travel. Nevertheless, he later carried out twelve more readings in London, when staying in his London home: his last was on 15 March 1870, when he read from *A Christmas Carol* and *The Pickwick Papers*. He had to cancel many appointments, though he managed a half-hour meeting with Queen Victoria in March and breakfast with Prime Minister Gladstone in May. All this time he

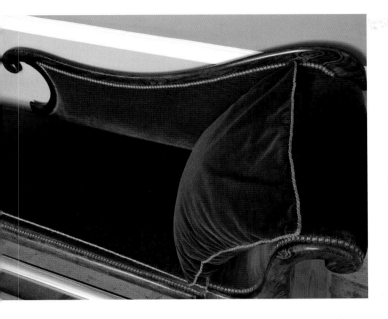

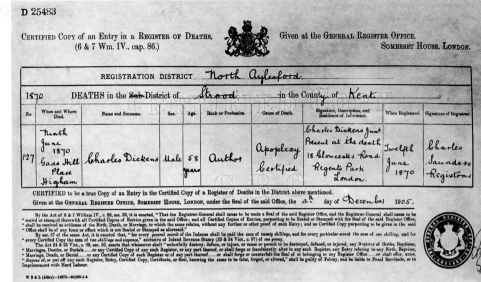

LEFT The couch at Gad's Hill Place upon which Dickens died on 9 June 1870, now in the Charles Dickens' Birthplace Museum in Portsmouth.

RIGHT The certificate of Dickens's death: the cause of death is given as apoplexy.

A brilliant morning shines on the old city. Its antiquities, and ruins are surpassingly beautiful, with a lusty ivy gleaming in the sun, and the rich trees waving in the balmy air. Changes of glorious light from moving boughs, songs of birds, scents from gardens, woods and fields – or rather, from one great garden of the whole cultivated island in its yielding time – penetrate into the Cathedral, subdue its earthy odour and preach the Resurrection and the Life. The cold stone tombs of centuries ago grow warm; and flecks of brightness dart into the sternest marble corners of the building, fluttering there like wings.

These were almost the last words he wrote.

Against his usual practice, he went back to work in the chalet in the afternoon; or, perhaps he went to Peckham to see Ellen,

as it has been convincingly argued. What is certain is that that evening he suffered a stroke and the following day he died on the couch in the dining room, which is now in the Birthplace Museum in Portsmouth. It was 9 June 1870, exactly five years after the Staplehurst railway accident that had so shocked him. As the page boy Isaac Armatage recounted many years later, his family gathered around him, with armfuls of flowers and letting the sunlight from the conservatory stream in.

THE LEGACY

Charles Dickens's wish had been to be buried in Kent. His friend and biographer John Forster reported his desire to end up in the little burial ground by the wall of Rochester Castle: 'There, my boy, I mean to go into dust and ashes.' His elder daughter, Mamie, said that 'on walks to Shorne, one of his favourite walks, he often said he would like to be buried there, by the quaint old church'. The Dean of Rochester Cathedral was expecting him to have a grave there.

But his immense status demanded that he be buried in Westminster Abbey. *The Times* said on 13 June that it was the only fit resting place for 'the remains of a man so dear to England'. So on 14 June he was interred in a spot selected by Dean Stanley of Westminster. Dickens did, however, have some of his desire granted, in the simplicity of the service. In his will he had written: 'I emphatically direct that I be buried in an inexpensive, unostentatious, and strictly private manner; that no public announcement be made of the time and place of my burial; that at the utmost not more than three plain mourning coaches be employed; and that those who attend my funeral wear no scarf, cloak, black bow, long hat-band or other such revolting

One of the last portraits of Dickens, a hand-coloured photograph taken in New York.

absurdity.' The funeral duly took place at 9.30 a.m. with only twelve mourners, after the grave in Poet's Corner had been dug at night. His name on the tombstone is, as stipulated, inscribed 'in plain English letters, without the addition of "Mr" or "Esquire"'.

The first bequest in his will (which had been drawn up in May 1869) was of £1,000 to Ellen Ternan. This was a bold gesture for someone who had been so private about his relationship, though the relatively small size of the bequest – out of an estate of £90,000 – might have been calculated to avert gossip. Ellen, no doubt amply provided for in other ways, discreetly faded into the background again. Six years later she married a schoolmaster, having knocked ten years off her age; she bore two children and died in 1914. By the oddest of coincidences, she is buried in the same cemetery as Dickens's first love, Maria Beadnell, at Highland Road in Southsea, a couple of miles from Dickens's birthplace.

Other bequests Dickens made were of his literary manuscripts to Forster; his books and prints to his eldest son, Charley, as well as his 'shirt studs, shirt pins, and sleeve buttons'; his jewellery 'and all the little familiar objects from my writing-table and my room' to Georgina, who was also awarded the largest bequest of £8,000. Provision was made for the servants (19 guineas to each with service of a year or more), and for Catherine, to whom he issued one last broadside: 'I desire here simply to record the fact that my wife, since our separation by consent, has been in the receipt from me of an annual income of £600, while all the great charges of a numerous and expensive family have devolved wholly upon myself.'

Exactly one month after his death, on Saturday 9 July at 1.00 p.m., his pictures were auctioned at Christie's. A sale of household effects took place at Gad's Hill Place between 10 and 13 August. The contents of the wine cellar selected by Dickens – 200 dozen bottles of wines, spirits and liqueurs – fetched £617 5s. 8d.; the rosewood grand piano from the drawing room, £28; the chalet furniture – two oak pillar claw tables, two muslin curtains and a cane seat – £2 10s. Gad's Hill Place itself was bought by Charley, and Mamie and Georgina went to live at 81 Gloucester Terrace, Bayswater, together with Dickens's sixth son, Henry.

The public mourned the loss of their favourite author, and within a very short time a Dickens industry sprang up. The first volume of Forster's *The Life of Charles Dickens,* published in the autumn of 1871, caused astonishment with the fact that the fictional account of David Copperfield's childhood was not so fictional after all (though Blundeston remained so). More books followed – biographies, reminiscences and (ironically, in view of Dickens's own attitude to destroying correspondence) collections of letters. Georgina and Mamie collaborated on one such, highly edited. Not only were certain letters omitted from the work, the first two volumes of which were published in 1880, but it is now clear from the twelve-volume Pilgrim edition of Dickens's letters that much of his correspondence to Georgina in his last years had been doctored: excisions of paragraphs or lines had been made and replaced with blank paper – presumably because they contained references to Ellen for, by the end, Georgina was also in his confidence.

There were the books on 'Dickensland', which had become a concept in his lifetime, with people following in his footsteps,

both real and fictional. What distinguished *A Week's Tramp in Dickensland*, published in 1891, was that the writer talked to people who had known Dickens. *The Philosophy of Dickens*, published in 1905, expounded on the use of Dickens as an adjective: 'People say now . . . of a neighbourhood, or a room, "How Dickens it looks", or "Do not alter your house – it is so Dickens".' The memorializing had begun in earnest. For example in Dover, as recorded in *The Dickensian* in 1908, a plaque was put up near a baker's by the market identifying 'the site of the steps on which Charles Dickens represents David Copperfield as resting in his search for his Aunt Betsey Trotwood'. In 1920, Broadstairs began labelling the houses in which Dickens had stayed.

At the start of the twentieth century, Percy Fitzgerald thought of forming the Boz Club, with pilgrimages and dinners to mark Dickens's birth and death. It started with 14 members, and eventually had 200, some 30 of whom had personally known Dickens. There is an account of an excursion on Saturday 9 June 1901 to 'Gad's Hill and Pickwick-land'. The group of enthusiasts was welcomed at Rochester by the Dean, who conducted them to the Bull Inn and then to the cathedral. A visit to the Guildhall was followed by a walk round the town, and then the group was driven to Gad's Hill by way of the Old Leather Bottle at Cobham. At Gad's Hill Place, the owner, Colonel Latham (who had apparently once received an offer of £10,000 to transfer the house to America), welcomed them to tea, and then they explored the house – the study, Boz's bedroom, the roof with its view – and walked through the tunnel to the spot where the chalet had stood in shrubbery. Then they went back to the Bull and dined in the ballroom where the dance in *The Pickwick Papers* took place. The tables were decorated with geraniums, Dickens's favourite flowers.

The Boz Club came to an end before the First World War, but in 1902 the Dickens Fellowship, with 6,500 members, was formed to 'knit together in a common bond of friendship lovers of the

The Pickwick Papers, set in and around Rochester, is remembered annually at the Rochester Dickens Festival, held each June.

great master of humour and pathos, Charles Dickens', to 'spread the love of humanity, to campaign against those "social evils" that most concerned Dickens'; and 'to assist in the preservation and purchase of buildings and objects associated with his name or mentioned in his works'.

The first opportunity to put this last objective into practice was in 1903, when the house where Dickens was born – which had been lived in by Sarah Pearce, daughter of John Dickens's landlord – came up for sale at auction. It was purchased by Portsmouth Corporation at the inflated price of £1,125 (the house next door sold for £625). It is thanks to the work of the first curator of the Charles Dickens' Birthplace Museum, Alfred Seale, that the couch upon which Dickens died was acquired, as well as what is perhaps the smallest possession: an elaborate mother-of-pearl waistcoat button. A large collection of souvenir ware indicates the calendars, plaques, plates, Toby jugs and figures of Dickens's characters that were churned out after his death. Initially, the museum housed a collection of books and periodicals by and about Dickens, but that was moved to Portsmouth Library, where a special room was created in 1976 for the Charles Dickens Collection.

In 1922, it transpired that 48 Doughty Street was in danger of demolition, as so many of Dickens's former abodes. Members of the Dickens Fellowship determined to buy it, raised a mortgage and bought the freehold in 1925, starting an appeal to pay off the mortgage and to furnish it. On 9 June 1925, the fifty-fifth anniversary of Dickens's death, the Dickens House Museum was opened. In 1926 the first brochure of the museum was published, at one shilling: a green pamphlet with a sketch of the house on the front, and on the inside cover an injunction to buy more copies: 'Emulate OLIVER TWIST – born in the Dickens House in 1837 – and ASK FOR MORE!' Listed inside were the presidents: Henry Dickens and Kate Perugini, as Dickens's daughter now was, and the vice presidents, a roll-call of the famous – Ellen Terry, J.M. Barrie, Jerome K. Jerome, Sir Arthur Conan Doyle, H.G. Wells, John Galsworthy. The brochure went on to announce that there was 'an attractive programme of Lectures, Recitals, Exhibitions and Dinners during the winter months and Pilgrimages to places connected with Dickens during the summer'. Cost of membership of the Fellowship – which entitled members to receive *The Dickensian*, a journal published three times a year – was half a guinea: 'Both Ladies and Gentleman are eligible for Fellowship.'

The membership branches then included – in London – Balham, Chiswick, Ealing, Hackney and St Pancras. There were altogether twenty-seven branches in England from Bath to Hull. Other branches were in Scotland (Edinburgh), Wales (Barry) and Australia, the USA, Canada and the Gold Coast in Africa. Now there are forty-eight branches throughout the world (and there is a Dickens Society in Boulogne), each one independent and arranging their own programmes of events. There is campaigning, too. In the 1960s, for example, residents of Blundeston wrote to John Greaves, secretary of the Fellowship for nearly thirty years, to ask that the government be prevented from building a prison in sight of the birthplace of David Copperfield. The Fellowship did not prevent that, but it has helped save other places connected with Dickens. Such work all requires a fair amount of fundraising, as with the decaying Swiss chalet.

The Charles Dickens Museum, as it is now called, faces new challenges of its own, and so launched 'Great Expectations', a fundraising campaign. In eighty years the house has had more than 2 million visitors and there are plans for extensive restoration and to develop the house next door (owned by the museum) as a visitor and learning centre for the bicentenary of Dickens's birth in 2012.

There have been other, smaller initiatives in former homes such as 'David Copperfield's Library for children', set up in 1922 in the Dickens family's former home at 13 Johnson Street in Somers Town by an American clergyman, the Reverend John Brett-Longstaff, but it lasted only a decade. But the most interesting prospect concerns Dickens's last home.

Gad's Hill School has, on occasion, been open to the public. There are still many of the features that were there in Dickens's day: the headmaster's study, with its dummy bookshelves, has a strong resemblance to Dickens's study. Opposite the front door, the tunnel with its twenty-one steps still leads down from the lawn (on which is a birdbath given by the Gad's Hill Preservation Society in memory of Cedric Dickens, a great-grandson, 'who loved this place'). In the hall, leaning against the wall, are two grave memorials, one for Dick, 'The Best of Birds; Born at Broadstairs Died at Gadshill Place 14 October 1866', (though this is a copy: the original is now in Philadelphia), and that of

Mamie's Mrs Bouncer, 'the most faithful, the most loving of little dogs'. Dickens's much-prized conservatory is now used as an overflow dining room; his bedroom with its far-reaching views, as an English classroom.

But this is all soon to change. The presence of 370 children in this historic building, headmaster David Craggs has said, is gradually stripping Dickens's home of its history. A new school is to be built in the grounds, and, with an eye on the bicentenary, the house will become a museum.

There is now, perhaps inevitably, a Dickens World, in Chatham, more or less on the spot where the family had its second home. Inside is a dim warren of cobbled streets, Dickensian inn yards, blackened walls and the Great Expectations Boat Ride. It avoids the Disney touch – just – with the accuracy of the information (advice was provided by the Dickens Fellowship) and the quality of its installations: the Dotheboys schoolroom with its desks and touch-screen snakes and ladders game on the novels; the 'magic lantern' show in Peggotty's Boathouse; the stage show in the Britannia

Theatre with animatronics – Pickwick on one balcony, Sam Weller on the other, and a believable Charles Dickens at his lectern. It is the sort of entertainment that Dickens himself might have appreciated, and on the wall is a quote from the circus manager Sleary in *Hard Times*: 'People mutht be amuthed. They can't be alwayth a learning, nor yet can't be alwayth a working.' There are, of course, many Victorian waifs, urchins and maids in attendance.

There is a lot of dressing up in Dickens's honour. All over the world there are Dickens festivals – at Riverside in California, Port Jefferson in New York State, Galveston in Texas and Holly in Michigan. The Charles Dickens Museum in Doughty Street opens every Christmas for an authentic Dickensian Christmas experience; even the museum director puts on a frock coat and joins in. The Broadstairs Dickens Festival, instituted in 1937 on the centenary of Dickens's first visit there, is in July, featuring plays and a procession of Dickens characters, helpfully grouped into novels and each labelled – though Miss Havisham in decaying wedding dress, Scrooge in nightcap and Magwitch in convict stripes probably need no introduction. They make their way down the main street to the greensward by the seafront, where in 2010 the local MP in a turquoise trouser suit introduced each character, one by one.

Rochester, which held a pageant in 1931 with '5,000 performers and special Dickens episodes', manages two festivals, one in June and one just before Christmas. Even the train guard is in on it: as the train pulls up at Rochester he announces: 'The next station stop is Rochester and the Charles Dickens Christmas Festival.' There are processions here too. One from the Royal Victoria and Bull Hotel is led by singing chimney sweeps to the Six Poor Travellers house, outside which a turkey is carved and distributed as in Dickens's story of 'The Seven Poor Travellers', with a man in a top hat summoning 'all poor people' to sample it. The Grand Parade brings a cast of Dickens characters, with a sprinkling of snow from a snow-making machine at the crossroads, on its way to Rochester Castle. There are readings, performances of *A Christmas Carol* and *Olivia not Oliver*, and a twelve-minute dramatized version of *Great Expectations*.

There are also guided walks, but you can do one of these yourself with the leaflet 'A Walk in Dickens's Footsteps'. This takes you past the cathedral and castle via the Guildhall, which Pip in *Great Expectations* thinks 'a queer place' with 'higher pews in it than a church' when he is brought here by Mr Pumblechook to be bound over as an apprentice to Joe Gargery (in another part of the Guildhall is the Dickens discovery room and the Hulk Experience, an effective reconstruction of a prison ship); the timber-framed mansion that featured as Mr Pumblechook's house; Eastgate House, Miss Twinkleton's 'seminary for young ladies' and Mr Tope's house (now a restaurant), both in *Edwin Drood*; and the Royal Victoria and Bull Hotel, which, since being taken over by new owners, has jettisoned all signs referring to Dickens and *The Pickwick Papers*, preferring instead to concentrate on its royal connection, with Queen Victoria's Chamber (complete with 'four poster bed, whirlpool bath, etc.'). Perhaps the new owners were eager to separate fiction from reality.

Fiction and fact are likely to be confused at Restoration House, an Elizabethan mansion so called because Charles II stayed here on his journey to London after his exile, and on which Dickens based Satis House, the home of Miss Havisham in *Great Expectations*, with its 'seared brick walls, blocked windows and strong green ivy'. There is no evidence that Dickens actually went inside the house, but the intricate connection of staircases and rooms fits well with his description of Satis House (a name he took from the nearby home of MP and philanthropist Sir Richard Watts). The Great Chamber of Restoration House, though it is now full of light and has had its panelled walls beautifully restored to their original pale green, looks as though it could have been the model for Miss Havisham's room – and was, indeed, used as such in David Lean's 1946 film. 'Some visitors do want it to be like that, but few are disappointed by the reality,' said co-owner Robert Tucker. 'They are transported. It is a tribute to Dickens's power of description, but this is the accurate version of a literary creation.' The reason for visiting this exquisitely restored house and garden (open two days a week in summer months) should not be muddled with Dickens, though in one of the last sightings of him a couple of days before he died he was leaning against the fence of the Vines park, originally the priory vineyard of the cathedral and in Dickens's time a meadow (where Edwin Drood walked with his betrothed, Rosa Budd) and looking up at Restoration House. Perhaps it would also have featured in *The Mystery of Edwin Drood*.

Licence is, of course, often taken. The Old Curiosity Shop in Portugal Street in London is a landmark but had nothing to do with the setting for the original (which was near Trafalgar Square).

LEFT The Great Chamber of Restoration House, the inspiration for Satis House, home of Miss Havisham in *Great Expectations*.

BELOW The Oriel Room at Restoration House.

Hotels trade on the connection, sometimes with a cavalier disregard for facts: according to its website, the (renamed) Royal Albion Hotel in Broadstairs thinks Dickens bought Bleak House. The Royal Hotel in Great Yarmouth announces that 'The famous writer Charles Dickens spent time at the Royal Hotel whilst writing the novel *David Copperfield*.' He didn't actually start the novel until later that year.

Restaurants and shops are named after him with scant attention to relevance, as in Broadstairs, for example: Marley's Coffee Bar, Pickwick Carpets, Barnaby Rudge restaurant, Nickleby's Takeaway on the corner of Dickens Way. There used to be a restaurant called Dickens in India; there is still one called Dickens Thai Diner . . .

But the real England of Dickens's time is still recognizable, in Broadstairs, Rochester and especially London. Some of the inns he wrote of still exist: the Boot Tavern in Cromer Street, headquarters of the Gordon Rioters in *Barnaby Rudge*; the George and Vulture chop house in the City, headquarters of Mr Pickwick; the George Inn in Borough, which appears in *Little Dorrit*. Sometimes his fictional characters have their own memorials, such as the plaque marking 'Nancy's Steps' from *Oliver Twist* on the south side of London Bridge.

The bicentenary of Dickens's birth in 2012 will be marked all round the world by celebrations, festivals, theatre productions and film and television retrospectives. Organizations including museums, libraries, universities and writers' groups will be taking part with displays, exhibitions and educational initiatives – for example, the launch by the Authors' Licensing and Collecting Society of a package on copyright education for use in schools called 'What the Dickens is copyright?'

In 2005 an additional objective was added to the constitution of the Dickens Fellowship: 'to promote the knowledge and appreciation of his work'. Perhaps there was anxiety that this was fading away in favour of *Oliver the Musical*. The bicentenary will certainly have played its part in reaching that objective. But it is

hard to believe it is necessary now when films and adaptations of his work crop up almost every week. *A Christmas Carol* was first filmed in 1901, and each of his novels has been filmed or televised, at least twice. When his work is parodied by *The Simpsons* and *The Muppet Show*, and when there are radio programmes such as *Bleak Expectations*, or *Charles Dickens's iPod*, which recreated Dickens's favourite music and was broadcast on Christmas Day 2010, it cannot feasibly be argued that raising awareness is necessary. Charles Dickens seems to be embedded in our culture and consciousness.

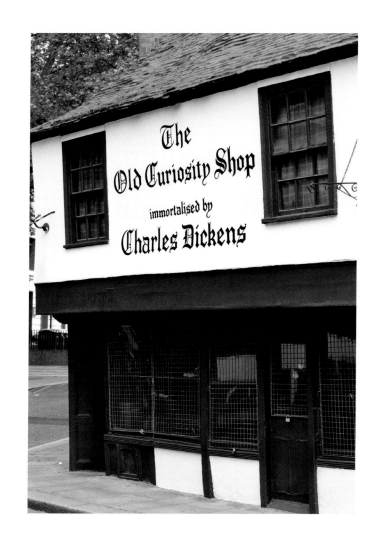

Every year thousands of tourists from all over the world come to London and the south of England to see the city and countryside that shaped Dickens. The comments in the visitors' book at the Charles Dickens Museum in Doughty Street – by visitors from Russia, Argentina, Australia – show the continuing impact of this man: 'We dreamt about it and now we are here'; 'I have waited half a lifetime to get here!'; 'Charles Dickens books are my life!'

Dickens and his novels live on in the names of businesses in London and in Rochester.

SELECT BIBLIOGRAPHY

Ackroyd, Peter, *Dickens* (Sinclair Stevenson, 1990)

Briggs, Asa, *Victorian Things* (Penguin, 1990)

Collins, Philip, *Charles Dickens: Interviews and Recollections* (Macmillan, 1981)

Dexter, Walter (ed.), *Letters of Charles Dickens*, 3 vols (Bloomsbury, 1938)

Dickens, Mary, *My Father as I Recall Him* (Roxburghe Press, 1897)

Dickens, Mary, and Hogarth, Georgina, *Letters of Charles Dickens* (Chapman and Hall, 1882)

Dickensian, The

Fields, James, *Yesterdays with Authors* (Sampson Low, Marston, Low and Searle, 1872)

Forster, John, *The Life of Charles Dickens* (Chapman and Hall, 1874)

Greaves, John, *Dickens at Doughty Street* (Hamish Hamilton, 1975)

Hartley, Jenny, *Dickens and the House of the Fallen Women* (Methuen, 2008)

Healey, Edna, *Lady Unknown* (Sidgwick and Jackson, 1978)

House, Madeline, and Storey, Graham (eds), *The Letters of Charles Dickens*, 12 vols, (Oxford University Press, 1965–2002)

Hughes, W.R., *A Week's Tramp in Dickensland* (Chapman and Hall, 1891)

Johnson, Edgar, *Charles Dickens: His Tragedy and Triumph* (Simon and Schuster, 1952)

Kitton, Frederic, *Charles Dickens by Pen and Pencil* (Sabin, 1890

Osborne, Charles, *Letters of Charles Dickens to the Baroness Burdett Coutts* (John Murray, 1931)

Slater, Michael, *Charles Dickens* (Yale University Press, 2009)

Storey, Gladys, *Dickens and Daughter* (Frederick Muller, 1939)

Tomalin, Claire, *The Invisible Woman* (Penguin, 1991)

Wilson, Angus, *The World of Charles Dickens* (Penguin, 1972)

FURTHER INFORMATION

Charles Dickens Museum
48 Doughty Street
London WC1N 2LX
tel. 020 7405 2127
www.dickensmuseum.com

Charles Dickens' Birthplace Museum
393 Old Commercial Road
Portsmouth PO1 4QL
tel. 023 9282 7261
www.charlesdickensbirthplace.co.uk

Dickens House Museum
2 Victoria Parade
Broadstairs CT10 1QS
tel. 01843 861232

Dickens World
Leviathan Way
Chatham ME4 4LL
tel. 01634 890421
www.dickensworld.co.uk

Guildhall Museum
High Street
Rochester
Kent ME1 1PY
tel. 01634 848717

The Historic Dockyard
Chatham ME4 4TZ
tel. 01634 823800
www.thehistoricdockyard.co.uk

Portsmouth Central Library
Guildhall Square
Portsmouth PO1 2DX
tel. 023 9281 9311

OTHER USEFUL WEBSITES

www.dickensfellowship.org
www.charlesdickenspage.com
www.historicmedway.co.uk

www.visitmedway.org

www.visitbroadstairs.co.uk

www.broadstairsdickensfestival.co.uk

www.rochesterdickensfestival.org.uk

INDEX

Page numbers in *italics* refer to illustrations

A

Albion Hotel, Broadstairs 66, 67, 68, 69, *69*, 73, 138
All the Year Round 7, 62, 89, 97, 98, 110, 111, 112, 113, 120, 125, 128
Alphington, Exeter 51–2, 78
America 7, 54, 76, 82, 91–3, 106, 107, 112, 127, 132
American Notes 7, 93
Andersen, Hans Christian 69, 83, 107, 119
Armatage, Isaac 106, 129
Austin, Henry 36, 78, 79–81, 82, 83, 84, 112, 116, 117, 119
Authors' Licensing and Collecting Society 138

B

Barnaby Rudge 7, 29, 35, 49, 54, 105, *106*, 138
Barnard's Inn 36
Barrow, Charles 14
Barrow, John 34
Barrow, Thomas 14, 29
Bath 73, 82, 134
Beadnell, Maria, 34, 36, 86, *86*, 116, 131
Beard, Thomas 41, 47, 57, 66, 68, 71, 73, 82
Beaucourt, Ferdinand 99, 100, 101
Belcher, George 106
Bentley, Richard 44, 49
Bentley's Miscellany 7, 44, 49
Birmingham Industrial and Literary Institute 7, 89
Birmingham Town Hall 89, *89*
Bleak House 7, 27–8, 29, 34, 36, 44, 69, 75, 77, *77*, 79, 83, 86, 95, 97, 99
Bleak House, Broadstairs 69, *70*, 71, 138
Blundeston 9–13, *10, 11,* 132, 134
Boulogne 78, *90*, 91, 99–101, 107, 116, 124, 134
Boyle, Mary 72, 84, 127
Brighton 72
Bristol 73, 82
Broadstairs 61, *64*, 65, 66–72, *67*, 73, 79, 81, 82, 93, 106, 110, 132, 134, 135, 138

Brown, Anne 73, 91, 92, 93, 104, 105, 106–7
Browne, Hablot (Phiz) 57, 65, 104
Bull Hotel, Rochester 23, 25, 126, 132, 136
Bulwer Lytton, Edward 108, 122, 125
Burdett Coutts, Angela 7, 58–60, *59*, 78, 85, 89, 94, 97, 100, 107, 108, 117
Burnard, Francis 101
Burnett, Henry 41, 50

C

Canterbury 118
Carlyle, Jane 56
Carlyle, Thomas 95
Cattermole, George 81
Cerjat, William de 10, 28, 97, 118, 122
Chalk 41, 43, 44
Chapman and Hall 43, 49
Charles Dickens' Birthplace Museum, Portsmouth 13–15 *12, 13,* 129, *129,* 133–4
Charles Dickens Museum, London 44, 50–1, *51,* 53, *53,* 134, 135, 139
Chatham 7, 9, 15–19, *15,* 24–5, 27, 30, 44, 87, 103, 115, 135
Chatham Dockyard 15, 17–19, *17*
Chatsworth 82, 99
Chester Place 61
Chimes, The 7, 75, 95, 108
Chorley, Henry 125
Christmas Carol, A 7, 29, 54, *55,* 84, 89, 127, 128, 136, 138
Cobham 116, 126, 132
Cobham Park 126
Cobley's Farm 66
Collins, Charles, 76, 119
Collins, Philip 12
Collins, Wilkie 57, 65, 68, 69, 72, 84, 85, 87, 99, 100, 101, 107, 111, 117, 121, 122, 124
Collins's Farm (Wyldes Farm) *48,* 49, 66
Condette *100,* 101
Cooling 18, *18,* 19, 112, 113, *113,* 120

Cooper, Benjamin 100, 106
Cornelius, Edward 107
Cornhill Magazine 76
Cornwall 65–6
Corsham 73
Couchman, Joseph, builder 122
Coutts Bank 83
Cowden Clarke, Mary 75
Cranford 82
Crewe, Lord 14, 103
Crewe Hall, 14
Cruikshank, George 44, 68
Cubitt, Thomas 81, 84

D

Daily News 7, 60, 61, 95, 96
David Copperfield 4, 7, 9–12, 16, 17, 24, 29, 30, 31, 32, 34, 35, 54, 62, 66, 69, 71, 72, 75, 78, 81, 115, 117, 120, 132, 134, 138
Devonshire, Duke of 83
Dickens House Museum, Broadstairs 71, *71*
Dickens, Alfred (brother) 30, 120, 122
Dickens, Alfred (son) 7
Dickens, Augustus (brother) 34
Dickens, Catherine (*née* Hogarth) 7, 28, 36, 39, *40,* 41, 43, *43,* 44, 47, 49, 50, 51, 52, 54, 55, 57, 58, 61, 62, 66, 69, 73, 75, 76, 79, 81, 82, 84, 85–6, 88, 91–2, 95, 97, 98, 106, 107, 110, 117, 119, 131–2
Dickens, Cedric (great-grandson) 134
Dickens, Charles *2, 33, 40, 80, 83, 84, 87, 95, 101, 120, 121, 125, 130*
and amateur dramatics 7, 56, 84–5, 86–7, *87*
and colour schemes 57, 58, 76, 78, 82, 84, 85, 96, 126
and conjuring 56
and dogs 106, 119, 121, 125
and furniture, 44, 51–2 55, 59, 65, 68, 71, 75, 77, 82, 85, 97, 98, 100, 118, 120
and games 16, 62, 66, 119, 125, 127

and homes (in chronological order), as a child:
    Mile End Terrace, Portsmouth *12, 13*, 13–15
    Ordnance Terrace, Chatham 16–17, *15*
    St Mary's Place, Chatham 17
    Bayham Street, London 28, *28*, 29–30, 51, 103
    Gower Street 30
    Little College Street 31, 32
    Johnson Street 32, 134
and homes (in chronological order), as an adult:
    Furnival's Inn 7, 35–6, 39, 43, 44, 47, 52, 55, 56, 103, 104
    Selwood Place 39, *41*
    Devonshire Terrace 7, 52–8, *53*, 60, 61, 62, 63, 66, 73, 76, 81, 82, 83, 91, 93, 95, 96, 104, 105, 106
    Doughty Street 7, 44–7, *45*, *46*, 49, 50–1, *51*, 52, 53, 55, 104, 111, *111*, 134, 135, 139
    Tavistock House 7, 76, 79–84, *79*, *80*, 85–6, 88, 89, 107, 110, 120
    Gad's Hill Place 7, 24, *25*, 75, *75*, 81, 82, 86, 88, 89, 107, 111, 112, 113, *114*, 115–29, *116*, *120*, *121*, *128*, 132, 134
and improvements and 'ingenious contrivances' 61, 100, 116, 117–8, 119, 121, 127–8
and letter boxes 57–8, 121
and order and tidiness 50, 65, 69, 75, 76, 83, 91, 120, 125
and public readings 7, 76, 89, 111, 124–5, *125*, 127–8, *127*
and ravens 105–6
and wallpaper 58, 62, 76, 120
and writing habits 44, 57, 65, 66, 68, 75–6, 97, 123, 129
and works *see individual titles*
Dickens, Charles/Charley (son) 7, 43, 44, 56, *56*, 60–1, 63, 88, 94, 117, 124, 131, 132
Dickens, Dora (daughter) 7, 63, 69, 107
Dickens, Edward/Plorn (son) 7, 85
Dickens, Elizabeth (grandmother) 103
Dickens, Elizabeth (mother) 12, 14, *14*, 15, 30, 52, 120
Dickens, Fanny (sister) 14, 19–20, 30, 31, 41, 50, 63, *63*, 106

Dickens, Francis (son) 7
Dickens, Frederick (brother) 30, 35, 36, 47, 91, 95, 106
Dickens, Henry (son) 7, 122, 132, 134
Dickens, John (father) 7, 12, 14, *14*, 15, 17–18, 24, 27, 30, 32, 34, 51, 63, 115, 133
Dickens, Katie/Katey (daughter) 7, 49, 52, 76, 79, 89, 100, 119–20, *120*, 128, 134
Dickens, Letitia (sister) 30, 36, 112
Dickens, Mary/Mamie/Mamey (daughter) 7, 49, 55, 63, 66, 76–7, 79, 85, 98, 99, 100, 101, 107, 111, 112, 113, 117, 119, 120, *120*, 121, 124, 125, 126, 131, 132, 134
Dickens, Mary Angela (granddaughter) 124
Dickens, Peter (great-grandson) 19
Dickens, Sydney (son) 7
Dickens, Walter (son) 7, 104
Dickens, William (grandfather) 103
Dickens Fellowship 132–3, 134, 135, 138
Dickens World, Chatham 135
Dickensian, The 16, 36, 51, 69, 132, 134
Dolby, George 125, 126, 127
Dombey and Son 7, 29, 31, 54, 60, 72, 76, 96, 97
Doncaster 87
Dover 16, 71, 72, 86, 132

E

East Anglia 12, 66
Eastgate House, Rochester 12, *12*, 23, 119, 122, 123, 136
Eeles, Thomas, bookbinder 82
Egg, Augustus 55, 84
Eliot, George 84
Evans, Frederick 88, 111

F

Fechter, Charles 122, 123, 128
Fields, Annie 112, 123, 126, 127
Fields, James 23, 29, 36, 112, 126
Fildes, Luke 75
Finchley 66
Fitzgerald, Percy 36, 101, 126, 132
Fletcher, Angus 93
Folkestone 65, 72–3, 101
Forster, John 15, 17, 27, 28, 31, 44, 49, 50, 52, 56, 57, 60, *60*, 63, 65, 66, 67, 69, 71, 73, 76, 91, 92, 93, 95, 96, 97, 99, 104, 106, 115, 117, 119, 131, 132
French, Charles 107–8

Frith, William 81
Frozen Deep, The 7, *84*, 85, 87, 88

G

Gad's Hill School 122, 134–5
Gaskell, Mrs 57, 82
Genoa 7, 54, 57, 75, 76, 93–5, *93*, 97, 104–5, 108
Giles, William, 24–5
Girardin, Emile de 98
Gladstone, William 128
Great Exhibition 78
Great Expectations 7, 16, 18, 19, 21, 23, 27, 29, 36, 41, 75, 113, 120, 136, 137
Great Ormond Street Children's Hospital 89
Great Yarmouth 9, 10, 13, 138
Greaves, John 134

H

Hard Times 7, 100, 135
Hedderley, Ellen 112
Higham 24, 115, 117, 128
Hill, Rowland 57
Hogarth family 39, 41, 85–6
Hogarth, George 34, 36, 39
Hogarth, Georgina/Georgie 7, 54, *55*, 61, 72, 75, 79, 82, 88, 95, 98, 101, 112, 119, 121, 124, 131, 132
Hogarth, Mary 7, 43, 44, 46, 47, 47–8, *47*, 49, 55, 66, 87, 95
Hogarth, Mrs 61
Homan, Franklin, cabinet-maker 122, 127
Household Words 7, 24, 29, 58, 59, 61–2, *61*, 62, 69, 72, 73, 75, 76, 82, 86, 87, 88, 99, 111
Huffam, Christopher 28
Hughes, William R. 54, 113, 119
Hugo, Victor 98
Hullah, John 43

I

Illustrated London News 76, 99
Isle of Wight 73
Islington 87

J

Jerrold, Douglas 86, 95
Johnson, William 113

K

Kent 9, 24, 27, 41, 66, 72, 115, 131
Kitton, Frederic 25, 53, 116, 118

CHARLES DICKENS AT HOME

L

Lamert, James 20, 30–31
Landseer, Edwin 106
Lausanne 7, 27, 28, 60, 76, 96–7, 108
Lawrence, D.H. 39
Leather Bottle, The, *see* Old Leather Bottle, The
Leech, John 10, 55
Lemon, Mark 10, 88, 117
Lewes, G.H. 51, 57
Lillie, Benjamin, decorator 54, 120, 122
Limehouse *1*, 28, 29
Lincoln's Inn *35, 95*
Little Dorrit 7, 31–2, 62, 73, 86, 96, 138
Liverpool 76, 91
London 7, 9, 14, 15, 25, 27– 37, 43, 44, 52, 60, 66, 68, 71, 87, 95, 97, 103, 107, 108, 115, 118, 120–1, 126, 128, 134, 136, 138, 139
Longfellow, Henry Wadsworth 49, 126
Lowestoft 9, 10
Lowestoft Journal 12

M

Maclise, Daniel 33, 43, 66, 71, 81, 91, 94, 95, 105, 106
Macready family 91
Macready, William 52, 95, 106
Macrone, John 34, 36, 41, 103
Manchester 7, 87, 88
Manchester Free Trade Hall 87
Marsh, James 106
Marshalsea prison 7, 30–2, *30, 32*
Martin Chuzzlewit 7, 31, 35, 36, 54, 66, 93
Martineau, Harriet 58
Master Humphrey's Clock 7, 49
MiddleTemple 35, 36, *37, 60, 61*
Mitton, Thomas 34, 52, 53, 57, 58, 61, 62, 68, 71
Mystery of Edwin Drood, The 7, 21, 24, 29, 34, 35, 36, 128, 136

N

Niagara Falls 49, 92, *92*
Nicholas Nickleby 7, 49, 52, 62, 65, 68, 125

O

Old Curiosity Shop, The 7, 31, 54, 58, 68, 103, 136
Old Leather Bottle, The, Cobham 126, *126*, 132
Oliver Twist 7, 44, 47, 49, *49,* 50, 51, 63, 65, 134, 138
Our Mutual Friend 7, 28, 29, 121–2, 124, 128

P

Paris 7, 60, 85, 86, 97–9, 100, 107, 111
Parker, David 51
Peckham 124, 129
Penny Illustrated Paper, The 101
Petersham 66
Pickwick Papers, The 7, 16, 23, 31, 41, 43, 49, 51, 67, *102*, 103, 104, *104,* 126, 128, 132, 133, 136
Pictures from Italy 7, 95, *96*
Portsmouth 7, 9, 13–15, 18, 115, 129, 133, 134

Q

Quennell, Peter 27

R

Restoration House, Rochester 136, *137*
Richmond 50
Roche, Louis 95, 104, 105, 108, 109
Rochester 9, 15, 20–4, *20, 21,* 25, 66, 87, 115, 116, 119, 121, 122, 123, 126, 128, 132, 133, 135, 136, 138, 139, *139*
Rochester Castle *8,* 23, *23,* 108, 119, 131, 136
Rochester Cathedral *8, 22,* 23, 131
Rochester Festival *133, 135,* 136
Rockingham Castle 97, 127
Rogers, Samuel 52
Royal Victoria and Bull Hotel *see* Bull Hotel

S

St Luke's Church *38,* 39
Scotland 7, 65, 66, 106, 134
Scott, Henry 112
'Seven Poor Travellers, The' 21, 24, *24,* 136
Shakespeare, William 54, 118
Sheerness 16, 18, 19
Shoolbred's, drapers 59, 82, 84
Sir John Falstaff, Higham 117, 118, *118*
Sketches by Boz 7, 34, 40, 41, *41,* 103
Slough 124
Smith, William, carpenter 82
Snoxell, William, blind-maker 53, 58
Southsea 15, 131
Stanfield, Clarkson 66, 94
Staplehurst rail disaster 101, *101,* 111, 124, 127, 129
Star and Garter hotel 50, *50*
Stone, Frank 76, 79–81
Stone, Marcus 76, 81, 83
Swiss chalet 122–4, *123,* 128, 129, 134

T

Tale of Two Cities, A 7
Tavistock House Theatre 84–5, *85*
Telbin, William, scene-painter 85
Ternan family 87–8
Ternan, Ellen 7, 87, 88, *88,* 99, 100, 101, 111, 121, 124, *124,* 129, 131, 132
Ternan, Fanny 87, *88*
Ternan, Maria 87, *88*
Thackeray, William 73
Thompson, Christiana 76
Thompson, John 57, 108–112, 118, 119, 120
Topping, William 105–6
Twickenham 66

U

Uncommercial Traveller, The 19, 24, 47, 115
Urania Cottage 7, 58–60, 78, 89

V

Victoria, Queen 128, 136
Village Coquettes, The 43

W

Warren's blacking factory 7, 31, 52, 103
Watson, Lavinia 10, 97, 112
Watson, Richard 83, 97
Watts, Sir Richard 24, 136
Weller, Mary 19–20, 103
Wellington House Academy 7, 32, 34
Westminster Abbey 131
What Shall We Have for Dinner? 62
Wills, William 61, 62, 76, 89, 98, 112, 113, 116, 117, 124, 125, 128
Wilson, Angus 95
Winter, Mrs *see* Beadnell, Maria
Winterbourne House 73
Wyldes Farm *see* Collins's Farm

Y

Yates, Edmund 121
Yorkshire 65

ACKNOWLEDGMENTS

AUTHOR'S ACKNOWLEDGMENTS

A book like this would not have been possible without access to libraries, public and private – from the extensive resources of the British Library to the dedicated collection of the Charles Dickens Museum. So I would like to gratefully acknowledge the part played by libraries everywhere.

I want to thank staff at the Charles Dickens Museum in Doughty Street, where my search began in the rooms of what was Dickens's home for three years: director Dr Florian Schweizer, curator Fiona Jenkins and librarian Don Staples. I'd also like to pay tribute to someone I interviewed there as a journalist in the 1970s, John Greaves, long-serving Secretary of the Dickens Fellowship, whose passion for Dickens remains vivid. I remember in particular his wistful comment when he found that I had not – then – read his favourite book, *Great Expectations*: 'I envy anyone who's reading that for the first time.'

Many others provided fascinating information, including Alan King of the Charles Dickens Collection in Portsmouth Library, and staff at the Charles Dickens' Birthplace Museum in Portsmouth and at the Dickens House Museum in Broadstairs. Without the enthusiasm and expertise of such custodians, fans of Dickens and his works would have a much thinner time. I would also like to thank staff at Gad's Hill School who arranged for me to visit: Sarah Garratt who organized it and Louise James who showed me round. Robert Tucker kindly invited me to join a private tour of the wonderful Restoration House in Rochester, a day that shines out in my research. Martin Yates lent me many books about Dickens from his impressive collection of Penguins. Staff at the Historic Dockyard and Dickens World in Chatham provided useful modern perspectives.

I have consulted many volumes of Dickens's letters, from early collections made soon after his death to the magnificent twelve-volume edition published by Oxford University Press: I would like to thank OUP and the Pilgrim Trust for permission to quote from *The Letters of Charles Dickens*.

I was asked by Andrew Dunn to write *Charles Dickens At Home* to accompany a great collection of photographs by Graham Salter, and so want to thank him for a project that proved so enormously interesting. Who would have thought that Charles Dickens had such strong views on colour schemes? Thanks too to Becky Clarke for her painstaking and imaginative design, Anne Askwith for her thoughtful and incisive editing, and Catherine Best for proofreading.

Finally, I'd like to thank Anna, Judith and Michael Shipman for their encouragement and support, as well as for pointing out interesting material (Anna), giving helpful advice at different stages (Judith) and being good company on visits to 'Dickensland' (Michael). Michael also read the final text, and was surprised to learn about Dickens's skill with the plum pudding trick.

PICTURE CREDITS

a=above b=below c=centre l=left r=right

Images © Graham Salter with the following exceptions:

p. 31, 60, 74, 80, 101 and front cover © The Charles Dickens Museum
p. 26 © Guildhall Art Gallery, City of London
p. 89 ©Birmingham Museums & Art Gallery

The photographer also wishes to thank the following individuals and institutions for permission to include photographs of their properties:

The Charles Dickens Museum (p. 14l, 14r, 40l, 40r, 43, 45l, 46a, 46b, 47, 51, 53l, 55l, 56, 59, 63, 68, 77, 83, 85, 86, 87, 88l, 106, 111, 117, 124, 125)
Portsmouth Museums and Records Service, Charles Dickens Birthhouse (p.2, 12l, 12r, 13, 120, 129l, 129r, 130)
The Dickens House Museum, Broadstairs, Kent (p. 4-5, 33, 67, 71, 104)
Rochester Guildhall Museum (p. 21a)
Heritage Officer, Medway Council (p. 21b, 122l)
The Dean and Chapter, Rochester Cathedral (p. 8, 22)
The Plough Inn, Blundeston (p.11)
The Honourable Society of Lincoln's Inn (p. 35)
The Honourable Society of Gray's Inn (p. 34l)
The Honourable Society of the Middle Temple (p.37, 61r)
The Rector, St. Luke's Church, Chelsea (p.38, 40b)
Gad's Hill School, Higham, Rochester (p 114, 123r, back cover)
Robert Tucker, Restoration House, Rochester, Kent (p.137a, 137b)

Every effort has been made to provide correct attributions. Any inadvertent errors or omissions will be corrected in subsequent editions of this book.